VIA FOLIOS 82

Lorenzo Del Boca

Polentoni
• The *"Polenta*-eaters" of Northern Italy •
How and Why
The North Has Been Betrayed

Translated from the Italian by
Ilaria Marra Rosiglioni

Library of Congress Control Number: 2012949793

Polentoni first appeared in Italian in 2011
published by
Edizioni PIEMME Spa
www.edizpiemme.it

Cover image used with the kind permission of Edizioni Piemme.

Printed in the United States.

Published by
BORDIGHERA PRESS
John D. Calandra Italian American Institute
25 West 43rd Street, 17th Floor
New York, NY 10036

VIA FOLIOS 82
ISBN 978-1-59954-055-9

Publisher's Note

"Polentone" is an offensive term used by people in southern Italy in order to describe those from northern Italy. With an etymology tied to the term "polenta" (ground yellow or white corn-meal), an English equivalent would be almost impossible to conjure up. "*Polenta*-eater," for sure, is a fine rendering in English. Likewise, "Cornball" might be close to another appropriate term in English. But neither really possess the derogatory socio-cultural foundation that "polentone" has in Italian. Not dissimilar to the various, negative epithets launched at Italian immigrants a century or so ago in this country ("dago," "wop," "guinea," "grease-ball," "spaghetti-bender," and the like), or toward Southern Italians in Italy, such as its counterpoint "terrone," "polentone" is often associated with that type of person who is ignorant, uneducated, and of poor hygiene usually suffering of pellagra, a vitamin B3 deficiency.

For this reason, we decided, together with the author, Lorenzo Del Boca, and the translator Ilaria Marra Rosiglioni, to maintain the original Italian title, *Polentoni*, for the English translation. We also opted to follow the Italian format in bibliographic references.

Finally, Bordighera Press acknowledges the kind generosity of the *Italian Language Inter-Cultural Alliance* (ILICA) in providing the necessary funds for the publication of this book.

TABLE OF CONTENTS

The "Polentoni" of the North Who Suffered the Risorgimento

"*L'Italie du nord est faite.... Il n'ya plus ni Lombardes ni Piemon- tais ... ni Toscans ni Romagnols....*" ("The Italy of the North has been established ... there are no more Lombards, Piedmontese, Tuscans, or inhabitants of Emilia Romagna....") On his deathbed, Camillo Benso, Count of Cavour, dictated his last will and testament to his nephew, William de la Rive, who was seated next to him. He did so in French.[1]

He seemed to be quite satisfied with the regions of the North. The Lombards, Piedmontese, Tuscans and inhabitants of the Emilia Romagna region all acknowledged their positions in the new State and gave the impression that they were willing to collaborate in order to reach common objectives.

"*Mais il y a encore les Napolitains....*" ("But we still have the Neapolitans....") The South, on the other hand, simply caused problems. The provinces of the former Kingdom of the Two Sicilies were in a revolutionary state. The brigands were increasing in number and grew progressively more dangerous. Even the liberals, who had initially welcomed the new order with enthusiasm, found their interest to be waning. Along the way, their enthusiasm simply ceased. Their words were filled with good intentions. Cavour excluded resorting to a state of siege as a possible solution. The South needed to be convinced and not forced to accept the notion of a Unified Italy. "*Je les gouvernerai avec la liberté ... pas état de siege....*" ("I will govern them with freedom and not with a state of siege....")

Sometimes details, despite their apparent triviality, render matters more immediately perceivable.

---

[1] William De La Rive, *Vita di Cavour*, Milan 1961.

Could Otto von Bismarck have expressed his final thoughts, I don't know … in English? Would it be conceivable for Abraham Lincoln to have expressed his thoughts as a statesman in Spanish?

The fact that Cavour, with his final dying breaths, spoke about Italy in French reveals much about the foundation of a State that did not even possess the cultural roots necessary to carry on its existence.

Ten years later, Francesco Crispi[2] appeared to be even more pessimistic. "Unfortunately, the seams with which the seven states were joined to form a single one have not disappeared altogether." Over time, the differences between the various regions have become amplified to the point that the traditions of each region have become incompatible with those of the others.

The anthem of Sicily promised certain disaster: "Against the tyrannical Italics/enemies of our land/each of us will take up weapons/shouting freedom….!" The score was composed by Vincenzo Bellini,[3] from Catania, and declared the need to free themselves quickly from the stifling regime that governed them from Rome.

One could easily line up the numerous poets and playwrights who, from the 14th century onward, entertained the idea of a nation held together by a common language. This, however, was merely a figment of their imagination based on hearsay rather than scientific evidence. By the middle of the 1800s, the Italian language was spoken by 1.8% of the population and, of that infinitesimal percentage one must also subtract those people who, like Cavour, preferred to express themselves in other languages.

But then again, one must ask, "What Italian language?" How does one go about explaining, as Ferdinando Petruccelli della Gattina attempted to do, a country that refers to a certain male anatomical part in the North as a "bird" and in the South as a "fish"?[4]

A single, unified Italy did not exist.[5]

---

[2] Francesco Crispi, *Carteggi politici inediti*, Rome 1901.
[3] The musical score was adapted by Giovanni Alessi Caterini.
[4] Enzo Biagi, *"I," come italiani*, Milan 1993.
[5] Aurelio Lepre, *Italia Addio? Unità e disunità dal 1861 a oggi*, Milan 1994

Charles VIII's troops, in 1494, crossed their Southern borders with bellicose intentions. They sang *"Nous conquerons les Italie."* They wanted to conquer the "Italies" and referred to Italy using the plural. If these multiple entities were unified at all in 1860, then it is due to "a literary miracle and the poetic inspiration of Napoleon III"[6]. This possessed only esthetic value, however, and served as a façade for a container with no authentic contents. It was formed without any true conviction.

The mere fact that "Unification" is declared does not automatically mean that it has actually been obtained. It was, in fact, quite the opposite as the original abstract notions that were used to justify its inception had actually weakened.

"Terroni"[7] and *"Polentoni"* have become the paradigm for distant worlds, sometimes at odds with each other and often hostile. At times, controversial disputes have escalated to verbal altercations. For example, Giorgio Bocca[8] held that "Naples is a city that has been in a state of decay for millennia. It is at the mercy of the commoners, dishonesty, and corruption. Since these appear impossible to defeat, they have overtaken the majority of the population." Could there be a possible solution? "The eruption of the Vesuvius....!"

A *terrone*, per se, was a farmer who tilled his land. This was hard work that took its toll on the farmer's back because the land is so low. It is for this reason that this profession was considered an honorable one, even noble. This word has now become an insult.

Likewise, a *polentone* was a valley-dweller who ate *polenta*:[9] almost exclusively polenta. He would have liked to place it beside a steak, but meat never seemed to make it onto his table. He would have appreciated a slice of salami but he could not find that either.

---

[6] Giustino Fortunato, *Il Mezzogiorno e lo Stato italiano:discorsi politici*, Bari 1911
[7] TRANSLATOR'S NOTE: People of the Dirt.
[8] Giorgio Bocca, *Napoli siamo noi*, Milan 2006. Further controversy was sparked due to the statements of the journalist when he was a guest of Fabio Fazio on the television program *Che tempo che fa* on February 24, 2010.
[9] TRANSLATOR'S NOTE: Cornmeal.

Perhaps it would have been sufficient to top the *polenta* with some tasty sauce but the only thing that could be found in homes at that time were poverty and children to feed. The *polentoni* and their descendants should look upon the effort required for survival with admiration. They should be proud of the social redemption of which they were protagonists. Their efforts have now become a fault that needs justification.

One only needs to surf the Internet amidst the blogs and forums to realize how quickly heritage and new prejudices become fast friends.

It is useless to complain that the 150th Anniversary of the Unification of Italy has become an engagement that one gazes upon with lazy negligence.

This is nothing in comparison to the enthusiasm in 1961, fifty years ago, on the occasion of the 100th Anniversary of the country's Unification.

For a century, Italy's history had been narrated by the victors whose only concern was to amplify their tiny virtues in order to magnify the defects of their adversaries. At school, the students were taught more lies than truths, and many facts were simply omitted. The students believed these lies and half-truths and therefore that their country had been the protagonist of an epic poem that was worthy of admiration and preservation.

Certainly there were those that expressed their disagreement but the few that did, did so behind closed doors.

Sidney Sonnino,[10] who was (in order) Minister of the Treasury, of Finance, of Foreign Affairs, and Prime Minister, declared: "If this is Italy, then it would have been better not to form it." Giovanni Giolitti, before Sonnino, agreed that "it would not be a good thing if the entire truth surrounding the *Risorgimento* was made known."[11] These were typical political "circle" topics of discussion that never went anywhere.

---

[10] Rolando Nieri, *Costituzione e problemi sociali. Il pensiero di Sidney Sonnino*, Pisa 2000.
[11] Alberto Acquarone, *L'Italia giolittiana*, Bologna 1988.

The others, those who were defeated during the *Risorgimento,* represented an absolute minority that was unable to even scratch, let alone dent, the cultural hegemony that governed it. The minority is a minority by definition: they are few in number with few opportunities to gain recognition and those that at that time possessed little means through which to communicate. The accusations of Alianello,[12] Molfese,[13] Pedìo[14] along with those of dozens of other local writers who dredged the archives to dig up uncomfortable truths were marginalized. Giacinto de' Sivo, who wanted to publish his own history of the Kingdom of the Two Sicilies with his own means, could not find a typographer willing to print his work because the content was unfavorable to those in power at the time. The diaries of Giuseppe Buttà were removed from libraries.[15] He was a military chaplain in the Bourbon army who accompanied his soldiers from Sicily to Gaeta. There is not even room for the stories of the Pro-Garibaldi commander Wilhelm Rustow,[16] who wore the "Red Shirt" while continuing to wear his brain. He had truthfully told the story of the *Mille* soldiers for what it was, with no frills or added miracles.

These are no longer those times.

No one believes that the "Savoy family only knows the way to exile and not the path of dishonor." It is impossible to recount this anecdote without raising a suspicion that borders hilarity. The defeated of the 1800s – the Southerners, brigands, proletariat, and the Church – picked their heads up and raised their voices. That which was not possible over the course of one hundred years became reality in the last twenty years through studies and research

[12] Carlo Alianello, *Alfiere,* Torino 1943; *Soldati del re,* Milano 1952; *La conquista del Sud: il Risorgimento dell'Italia Meridionale*, Milan 1994.
[13] Franco Molfese, *Storia del brigantaggio dopo l'Unità d'Italia*, Milan 1966
[14] Tommaso Pedìo, *Inchiesta Massari sul brigantaggio: relazioni Massari-Cotagnola, lettere e scritti di Aurelio Saffi , osservazioni di Pietro Rosano, critica della Civiltà Cattolica,* Manduria 1983; *Brigantaggio meridionale 1806-1863*, Naples 1987; *Il brigantaggio: un aspetto della grande tensione esistente nelle champagne*, Potenza 2002
[15] Giuseppe Buttà, *Viaggio di Boccadifalco a Gaeta*, Brindisi 2006.
[16] Wilhelm Rustow, *La guerra italiana del 1860 descritta politicamente e militarmente*, Milan 1862.

that became evermore numerous and supported by documentary evidence such that it caused serious dents in the credibility of the traditional "vulgate." The official historiography, however, was unable to handle these revisionist theories with the result being that the rift between the intellectual elite and the rest of the country has widened to the point where they are almost no longer reconcilable.

Amongst those who were defeated by the *Risorgimento* is the North, from which the entire Unification machine was set into motion. But the North, which took initiative in those twenty years from 1850 to 1870, was represented by a few hundred members of the bourgeoisie who were already in government positions, but with higher ambitions. The true North, that of the fields and the factories, not only kept itself out of the discussion, but also, in certain instances, showed that it was downright hostile towards the recent changes. When the war of independence ended, the North realized that it gained no benefits and that the State budget was in the red. Someone had to pay: them. Unfortunately, the tab is still open and the North continues to pay.

The *terroni* may even be right to make their claims. Did you know that they allege that at one time, they were the "North"? That the Piedmontese, from the moment of their arrival, took all that was possible? That from that moment onward, there was no other choice for a Southerner than to be a brigand or to emigrate?

The *polentoni* have many issues with which they can reply. Did you know – they explain – that the *Risorgimento* had more devastating effects for the North than if they had lost a war? That the war spoils wound up in the private coffers of a few patriots, leaving the rest empty-handed? The liberals who had just been converted, the begging martyrs, the last-minute volunteers all wound up on the payroll of the Treasury, which began emitting pensions, damages, refunds, and other provisions with such generosity, (while benefitting only a small percentage of the population) that transferred directly into the taxes imposed upon everyone.

Already in 1935, the clandestine pages of the *Giustizia e libertà*[17] periodical had sparked a debate in order to rid the history of various ideological "frills" and other incredible inventions regarding the country's history. Andrea Caffi began with his thought that "in order to have a clear and profound vision of the Italy of tomorrow" it is necessary, on one hand, to radically decline the "official, scholastic" version of the *Risorgimento* and, on the other hand, to re-evaluate Mazzini's idea.

Franco Venturi was very interested in this debate. He went by his pen name "Gianfranci." The issue also interested Umberto Calosso, the English historian Griffith, and Nicola Chiaromonte (who went by "Luciano"). The last word, however, went to Carlo Rosselli (whose pen name was "Curzio"). "The myth of the false *Risorgimento* must be repressed in respect to a *Risorgimento* myth that is pure and unadulterated, that is worth salvaging. Nevermind ignoring! We must still learn what there is to know about the *Risorgimento* and must study it further. We must fight against the official, scholastic, Piedmontese version of the *Risorgimento* in favor of that of the people: the revolutionary version that is still unknown to too many people. We must tear away the biased historical veils that taint it. We must be ruthless with the official version ... the moderate, Savoy, uncultured Italy that emerged from the *Risorgimento* has been a failure. Not only did it not resolve the problems that arose, for better and for worse, but rather eluded them through repression, inertia, and compromise. If we were to judge the *Risorgimento* by its results then we should toss the entire movement out."

Not only were there no great strides made, but we are still trying to answer those questions raised by Rosselli, Gramsci, and Proudhon who tried, unsuccessfully, to tell the true story to the common man.

---

[17]In the periodical *Giustizia e libertà* (founded in 1929) the first article appeared in the edition of March 25, 1935. In 1997, the entire collection of writings was published in a volume called *Unità d'Italia: pro e contro il Risorgimento* in the *Edizioni e/o di Roma* with a preface written by Alberto Castelli

We must celebrate this 150th Anniversary of the Unification of Italy. We cannot turn back and, unfortunately, we cannot change what happened. Anniversaries are what they are, and time itself acts as a reminder to us of this. But all of the heads of state, public authorities, institutional representatives, elderly converts, and inventors/exploiters of political debates should not expect any additional enthusiasm.

CHAPTER 1

Shall We Boil Italy Alive So That We Might Resurrect Her?

"I have never believed in the Unification of Italy. It is an idea that I have refused on principle and that I contest on the grounds of practicality. The vast majority of Italians is federalist and your unity, as you have constructed it, evokes feelings of pity and annoyance. We hate it and will not accept it for anything in the world."[1]

These are the words of Proudhon, as written in the *Messager de Paris* in the year of our Lord 1862, on the 13th of July.

Proudhon – Pierre-Joseph Proudhon, to be precise – conquered his position in the hall of fame of Leftist Revolutionaries where he was forced to accept some moral responsibility for having inspired the dictatorial experiences of the so-called "Soviet Royal Socialism."

"Property is theft," was a phrase that he uttered. He was a bright boy but his family could not pay for his studies. In order to study at the university, he was obliged to work at a printing company. He had tested on his own skin the weight of hard labor and understood the value of a monthly salary. Perhaps he had received some unjust treatment that brought him to harbor certain prejudices against the ruling class. It is probably for this reason that he declared that profit was immoral, unless it was acquired directly from the work of a worker or an artisan. He imagined founding a

---

[1] Pierre-Joseph Proudhon, *Mazzini e l'Unità italiana*, Bruxelles, July 13, 1862. Proudhon wrote another article with the title *Garibaldi e l'unità italiana* that was published on September 4, 1862. In 1863, the two articles, preceded by an introduction, were published by the Parisian publisher Dentu in a book called *La federazione e l'unità d'Italia*. Recently, another publication was proposed by Edizioni Mirangeli (Turin, Via Napione) with a preface written by Antonello Biagini and Andrea Carteny with the translation by Paola Goglio.

bank "of the people" that would have established a system of free credit in order to avoid the vile practice of dealing with money.

Now, those theories leave an acid taste in one's mouth because they are half-way between a Utopian ideal and a provocation. At that time, these notions were considered dangerous. Proudhon wound up in jail. He was arrested and accused of sedition and put on trial. In the end, he was acquitted but the books he had written were confiscated and banned. This did not, however, prevent him from influencing the world and becoming an icon for the political movements of the Left.[2]

Speaking of the Unification of Italy, even at home, Antonio Gramsci, the founder of the *Pci* (the Italian Communist Party) stated with a peremptory tone that the *Risorgimento* was branded by the bourgeois and business. It was not a movement done by the people, who had never participated to the events surrounding the Independence movement, but was rather the business of bankers and large industries who cared little about the principles of freedom because they were too busy trying to profit from what they were building. He grew up in Ales, in Sardinia, but his family was of Southern Italian descent. His father, Giuseppe, was born in Gaeta in 1860, just in time to witness the Kingdom of the Two Sicilies. His grandfather, Gennaro, held the title of *"don"* and had been a captain of the Bourbon police force.

As a serious Communist, he did not forget his Southern roots. His comments regarding the conquests of the Piedmontese and Garibaldi's project leave no room for interpretation. "The Italian State," he writes, "was a fierce dictatorship that greatly tested the South and the islands by crucifying, quartering, and burying alive the poor farmers that the Sardinian writers attempted to defame and brand with the name 'brigand'."[3]

Nationalism, which places great value on one's homeland and the heroism of those who sacrifice themselves for its glory, has always been a practice of the Right. On the other hand, the Left

---

[2] Giampietro Berti , *Volume antologico degli scritti di Proudhon*, Milan 2006.
[3] Antonio Gramsci, *Il Risorgimento italiano*, Rome 1991.

preached "internationalism": the proletariat should not see any distinctions between man-made geographical borders but rather see all as equals and march together towards the future. Nationalism, because it builds hierarchies of values in different States, needed to be fought because it created false objectives and distracted the people from the path that they needed to all walk down, side by side, as equals.

The only flag that should be flown was the red one with the hammer and sickle that recalled the realm of the worker. All the others – even the Italian tricolor flag – were considered Fascist. In fact, the post-Fascist Italian social movement, at the moment of its inception, distinguished itself by using a tricolor flame. It was Enzo Bearzot who in 1982, on the occasion of the Italian victory of the World Cup, waved the flag of our home that, from that moment onward, obtained a popularity that had been suspended if not denied.

It is comprehensible that still today, the heirs of the Right remain firm on certain issues. It is amazing that, for sixty years, it harbored a sort of neglectfulness towards symbols of the State and has now become their most fervent supporter. It elicits peals of laughter when they are outraged by those who have a different view. In order to correct the country's history, as is most convenient, they deny their own history and in so doing, they go beyond what is allowed and border the confines of ridiculousness.

Music and sports have also participated in this tiresome debate.

Music: Sandro Cappelletto held that one must not play Radetsky's March because it was composed as an ode to an Austrian general as he returned to Milan after having defeated those who fought in the Five Day Insurrection.[4] Bizzarre. Perhaps we should then re-examine Giuseppe Verdi's *Va' pensiero*. Verdi was the physical embodiment of patriotism. His name was used as an acronym for "Victor Emanuel King of Italy." When the *Scala* theater in

---

[4] Sandro Cappelletto, *Con Radetsky non c'è nulla da festeggiare*, in *La Stampa*, December 28, 2010.

Milan presented his opera *Nabucco,* the Lombards chimed into the chorus singing "Oh my homeland, so beautiful and lost..." in defiance to the Austrians in the theater, who responded by leaving.

Sport: The successes of athletes have always been used by the State to glorify itself. Mussolini's World Cup...Hitler's Olympics ... soccer even held together the troops in both Brazil and Argentina.... How come now the Left has begun to root for the national soccer team? Why is it that now tepid cheering is censored and branded as an insult?

Now Valentino Rossi races with a Ducati motorcycle and his fans can rest easy. But what about when he raced for Yamaha and Ducati was in the hands of Stoner? How could one be Italian then?

History has no color, and therefore cannot be "tricolor." The past, and therefore our past as well, cannot be the propagation of various episodes that have been purposely embellished to be more beautiful, heroic, and admirable than what actually happened. Confusing what is real with what was probable and recounting what would have been nice to have happened as though it actually happened is a disservice to the knowledge of yesterday, today, and tomorrow.

The past, and therefore our past as well, is, whether we like it or not, what it is. Trying to hide the worst of it amidst the verbose pages of books is equivalent to sweeping dust under the carpet. Mistakes should be highlighted so that they can serve as lessons on what is to be avoided in the future. This would allow for a general improvement in both public and private life.

Proudhon's criticisms on the Unification of Italy do not come from a reactionary, bigot, pro-Pope, or Bourbon-favorable person. They are the words of a revolutionary who, without having his eyes shielded, managed to preserve a certain honest intellectual lucidity so that he might accurately judge what was happening around him. He managed to declare his thoughts clearly, without censoring himself.

In 1848, when Europe was on fire due to the many revolutions taking place, Proudhon was standing amidst the barricades in Paris. In June of that year he was elected a deputy to the Assembly.

The French Parliament did what it could to assist the libertarian movements in Italy despite the conditions in which it found itself. France expressed its solidarity and even admiration towards the Five Day Insurrection in Milan, the Republic declared in Rome, and the Venetians that rebelled against the Austrian domination.

This was short lived. The old regimes were reinstated and Proudhon fled to Belgium, which was more tolerant and hospitable, in order to avoid further problems with the law due to his political beliefs.

From that observation point, he was able to closely follow the *Risorgimento* which elicited some poisonous comments from him. "When the Unification is enacted, the Italian population will most certainly not be better off!"[5]

He openly disputed Garibaldi. He did attribute to Garibaldi the courage of a lion, but he criticized the "hero of two worlds" for his gladiatorial poses and despised his exaggerated efforts to be well-liked. "We honor Garibaldi as a fervent patriot even though he has often been misunderstood. We respect the injury he received in Aspromonte but dear God! Let us not make a relic of this injured leg!"[6]

Proudhon liked Mazzini even less, although he should have had an affinity with Mazzini's character given the radicalism of his own spirit: "He asked that Victor Emanuel, without any scruples towards the rights of the people, the principle of nationalism, the interest of the people, of the true spirit of the revolution and certainly not towards the monarchy's needs, take possession of the various states of the peninsula."

These were grim predictions. "The first effect that the new centralization will have is to ensure the disappearance of any local characteristic flavors in the various places in the country. The objective of this action is to highlight the political inclinations of the masses. Instead, what is accomplished is the destruction of its constituent parts through to their very core. A state with twenty-

---

[5] Giampietro Berti, *Volume antologico degli scritti di Proudhon*, Milan 2006.
[6] Pierre-Joseph Proudhon, *Contro l'unità d'Italia*, Turin 2010.

six million souls is a state in which every municipal and provincial freedom is confiscated to the advantage of a higher power that is the State. Each small town must be silent. Local pride must be quelled. The community is absorbed by the central power. First, one appeals to nationalism and the first action after the independence movement is to engulf it: Neapolitans, Romans, Lombards, and Tuscans are no more in Italy than the Hungarians, Bohemians, and Croatians are in Austria.... This is a sensational contradiction, a derision of the individual, and a disappointment for a project that is destined to die."

How should the new citizens be governed? With much disapproval, Proudhon watched as the government entities of the first, second, and third degree grew without offering additional services and without promoting improvements to the quality of life: "In order to render this enormous machine operational," he maintained, "it is necessary to have a prodigious bureaucracy and legions of civil servants. In order to properly defend this system, from both the inside and outside, and to render it respectable by its subjects and adversaries, a permanent army is necessary." Therefore: "Employees, soldiers, and taxes...this is what will substitute the nation from now on. The State's general expenses will increase in proportion to the centralization and will be inversely proportionate to the freedom granted to the provinces. To this grand Unification, lastly, glory, prestige, and luxury are necessary. An imposing appanage follows ... sumptuous treatments ... encouragement towards literature and the arts ... missions ... pensions ... sinecures.... Those who are ambitious, intriguing, the decadent, the *Bohèmiens* and all who are supporters of the Unification swarm around the new government. Everyone extends their hands in asking and one cannot give everything to one group and nothing to the others. It is necessary to remember the towns, the parishes, and the brotherhoods with gifts, subsidies, and commissions.... Many projects are commissioned to embellish the nation. Buildings are constructed and demolished. Monuments to local heroes are erected. Decorations, exhibits, reductions, supply contracts, mines, canals, colonies, agencies, and concessions are the currency that the government uses to repay their supporters. They allow everyone to sample the wealth. Everyone competes to "get a bigger piece of the pie." There are those who declare that a unified nation is a "sold" nation ... *urbem venalem....*"[7] There is no scarcity of examples. "One can buy a city with a Church and a town with a tobacco shop. I saw the capital of a district punished by retiring the infantry regiment that was stationed at the city's garrison. I saw someone deny their opposition for a position as a police commissioner."[8]

The only ones who actually gained any benefits from the Unification were those members of the ruling bourgeois class, who were naturally supporters of the independence movement and consequently first in line to reap the rewards. "An excess of politics carries one outside the realm of politics. Squandering and deficit, abuse, hypocrisy, tyranny, subordination, fire, massacre, and ruin: these are what Italy has reaped in the last four years from Mazzini's politics. His methods have been adopted by Cavour, supported by France and by a press that exerts no authority." Even more severe: "Mazzini merely participated in the "Gold rush." In his lifetime, he only knew how to do two things: suck money and blood from the population. In the end, however, how much were his friends able to gain, those men "of the people"? In that case, we are no longer speaking of union, but of coercion."

It was inevitable that a series of controversies would ensue. Proudhon picked up his pen once again in order to quell the notions of several journalists "amongst which it is only necessary to cite Monsieur de Girardin, who was called upon to bring about the disapproval of the liberal public upon me."

In order to demonstrate his theory, he took a roundabout route and cited historic events that had been dead and buried for millennia.

---

[7] TRANSLATOR'S NOTE: A quote by Jugurtha, King of Numidia: *"urbem venalem et mature perituram, si emptorem invenerit"* which, from the Latin means, "a city for sale and doomed to perish soon, should it find the right buyer")
[8] *Ibidem.*

"If you begin at the mouth of the Nile River and proceed around the Mediterranean, coming back through Syria, you will only encounter free countries. Freedom is a gift of the sea because it is the sea that renders cities independent by forcing slavery further inland together with the great dominions. Asia Minor is almost entirely composed of small city-states that can be found in the mountains, at the mouths of rivers, and whose base is on the sea. If one crosses the Bosporus a similar site comes into view upon seeing Greece from Byzantium to Corfu. Where do the vast empires that delight intellectuals and children, without teaching anything to either, lie? On the mountain chains that are separated by large rivers. In this case, it is an expression of dependency rather than freedom. One can cite Egypt as an example and Assyria, which lies between the Tigris and Euphrates Rivers along with Persia.[9]"

The posthumous confirmation of this theory comes from the fact that the "land between two rivers" is occupied today by Iran and is ruled by that champion of tolerance known as Mahmoud Ahmadinejad who would rather see all the continents fight so that he might be rid of the Jews, Americans, the Westerners, and even the Arabs who do not bend to his every whim. "Xerxes ordered the scourge of the Hellespont which serves as an allegory of a despot who violates Aphrodite, the goddess of the sea and freedom."

"Most of the time, the services rendered to the world are inversely proportionate to the vastness of an empire. What do we have left of the Babylonian Empire? What did the Chaldeans leave behind? Not much. However, Judaea, the Phoenicians, and the Greeks with their islands left behind an enormous legacy: philosophy, art, architecture, writings, politics, industry, religion, laws. Egypt can boast that it invented navigation, but it was the Phoenicians and the Greeks who used it to explore the world."

Proudhon's theory continues on without trepidation and once in a while plunges into the depths of logic, never losing sight of its objective.

---

[9] *Ibidem.*

What about Italy? "Italy is a long peninsula that is divided lengthwise by a mountain chain that counts numerous valleys on either side of it. It has numerous crests that are perfectly independent. It resembles the skeleton of a large cetacean. This construction is one of the most original and decidedly federalist structures in the entire world. These tiny areas are so close that they could rely on benefit associations but are also independent enough to have no need for such binding ties." How does one go about unifying these cities? "What need is there to unite, under the same government, Sicily and Sardinia? What need do these islands have for one another, or for the neighboring mainland, for their security, agriculture, or industry? Only commerce could justify their annexation but commerce, which is the second most important activity after labor, is that entity which least requires centralization. Isn't there free exchange? There could be at least sixty kingdoms created in Italy! After all, this is how Italy survived for many centuries prior to the Roman conquest and after the fall of the empire, it returned to this natural state. Summed up, that amounts to one thousand years."

There is only one lesson to be learned. "It is evident that Italy is Anti-Unification."[10] What interest do the proponents of this movement have that prompts them to pressure their fellow countrymen to adopt this oft contradicted notion? It has been contradicted time and again by geography, tradition, nature, and history. This is arbitrariness's conspiracy against freedom."

The only explanation is that too much invested interest and corrupt business hides behind the *Risorgimento*.

"The movement to unify Italy has become a government clique. The clique is a product of the politics of business. If we want to call it by its true name, it is called corruption. Unification, therefore, equals centralization, big salaries, plum positions, monopolies, privileges, concessions, and gratuities."

Proudhon summarized the issues that Italy would have to face and arranged them in an outline format, beginning each line with

---

[10] *Ibidem.*

a dash and an asterisk in order to give each line its due importance.

Whoever believes that unification also means centralization must know that they are also addressing:

- the business world
- centralization of funds
- centralization of credit, anywhere from 7 to 10%
- centralization of mortgages, reinstatement of large properties, dominions, feuds, and estates
- alliance of the bourgeois with the centralized State along with all of the land-owning, financial, and profiteering aristocracy
- hoarding of state loans
- industrial and mercantile feudalism
- increase in taxes
- increased jobs
- increase of the public debt[11]

It seems like an understatement to say that Proudhon was right regarding the past, present, and even what seems to be the future. His thoughts are still current. There is no hint of leniency in his prose.

The Unification would mean to go against the nature of an entire country, de-nationalize ten different populations, and arbitrarily transform twenty-five million souls with complete disregard to their land, race, and ideas. That false liberalism could conceive of such a project is comprehensible. However, I continue to be surprised by the fact that true patriots allowed themselves to be duped with such Machiavellian tactics. Have you ever seen a doctor try to cure a patient by performing an autopsy? Italy uniting under the sceptre of one king reminds me of the myth of Aeson, whose daughters boiled his body to rejuvenate him.[12]

---

[11] *Ibidem.*
[12] *Ibidem.*

CHAPTER 2

It Would Have Been More Convenient to Buy Italy Rather Than Free It!

Why was the damage from the earthquake in Friuli repaired while that in Belice was left as evidence of the disaster?

Why was the evidence left behind by the flood in Florence (and that of Biella) quickly canceled while some towns in Irpinia are still uninhabited?

Why is it that in the Veneto region, life resumed normally after the flood when the President of the *Confindustria,* Andrea Tomat, only asked to use local tax funds to repair the damage while Messina, Basiicata, and Calabria merely sent a long list of expectations to Rome?

Sometimes the requests have no clear motives behind them. Capistrello,[1] a town in the Abruzzo region, had no damage from the earthquake and yet it obtained, with its population of around 5000 people, 275,000 Euro for its schools, 80,000 Euro for its main road, 50,000 Euro for the roof of its Church, and 150,000 Euro each for its new soccer field (complete with Astroturf!), new town hall, new station for its *carabineri,* and a new sewer system. This money all came from specially allotted government funds.

Why was the North able to build landfills, incineration plants, and arrange for door-to-door garbage pick-up while the South, with the same funds and tax money available (and in some cases more funds) was only able to build one waste disposal site in the town of Acerra?[2]

---

[1] *A Capistrello la Margherita fa miracoli–Fondi ai terremotati,* in *Panorama,* November 11, 2010.
[2] Domenico Tempio, *Ma la lega (purtroppo) ha ragione,* in *La Sicilia,* November 21, 2010.

Why complain that Naples is drowning in garbage if the refuse collectors call a strike precisely when the emergency situation reaches a critical point? Why is the national average weight of recycled refuse 50 kilograms per person when in the Campania region that average barely reaches 24 kilos? Barely *reached* ... in the last few months, since the problem has worsened, the participation rates have dropped, and those 24 kilograms are a distant memory.[3]

The answer and solution to all of these questions is federalism.

Umberto Bossi has made it his business to promote this concept and it has acquired a permanent place on his political agenda. Some have understood little of what it actually means and some have not understood this concept at all. Regardless, this issue has become unavoidable.

Let us proceed from mere words to facts.

On April 29, 2009, the Senate approved the bill on fiscal federalism and the government proceeded to make it a law. We began with federalism of the State and the process was completed by establishing a new so-called municipal federalism.[4] The era of diverted finance had come to a close. This means that local governing bodies no longer have to go to Rome to beg for funds, but rather have to organize themselves on the basis of their own abilities and with their own resources that they manage to amass. Those who are behind will have to carefully watch their spending because they will no longer receive assistance based on their spending but rather on the effective cost of the services.

Now the differences are too great and there is great inequality in the distribution of the wealth. Half of the country has their sleeves rolled up trying to keep up with all of their work, trying to increase production and improve their yield while the other half lives off of their income, barely getting by, while waiting for an improbable miracle.

---

[3] Giuseppe Marino, "Napoli ultima vergogna, nel 2010 è diminuita la raccolta differenziata – Da inizio anno in calo la carta riciclata e la cartiere campane sono costrette a importarla da altre regioni," *Il Giornale*, October 28, 2010.
[4] *Atti Parlamentari,* May-June 2009.

In the North, a pouch of blood costs about 3 Euro. In the South the cost can reach up to 10 Euro. Why is this? The best hypothesis remains that the higher prices serve to "make up for" the laziness in the inspections and the inefficiency of the organization. Certainly it is not rare (who would deny it?) that around the health-care expenses, which are usually the most important aspect of any government administration, a parallel economy develops that involves friends and friends of friends. The inflated expenses increase the power of the clientele and foster the development of a spoils system, unjustified employments, disproportionate hiring and personnel organization (in order to please various persons), and jobs assigned to more people than necessary in the hopes that at least one of the employees will carry out the assigned task.

For example: in Basilicata, the Attorney of the State placed the heads of the regional council under investigation. They were suspected of having "fixed" a subcontracting bid that would assign the cleaning crew, porters, and meal assembly for the hospital in Potenza. This deal was worth twenty-five million Euro.[5]

How about another example? In Umbria,[6] the local company that manages the healthcare providers, Unit 3 located in the city of Foligno, is in a state of turmoil. The magistrate is currently monitoring the rapport amongst the personnel that works in the public healthcare division as well as those employed in private hospitals. The magistrate fears that there are illegal liaisons between private operators and the public administration.

How about yet another example? In Brindisi,[7] twenty-four people were arrested including doctors, nurses, and laboratory technicians. They validated their time cards in the healthcare institutions where they were hired but then they went to work somewhere else. They were caught by video camera surveillance.

---

[5] Emanuela Fontana, "La sanitopoli nella Basilicata rossa: appalti truccati, nei guai I vertici Pd," *Il Giornale*, December 24, 2010.
[6] "Grande frana nell'Umbria – Una serie di scandali nella sanità rischia di travolgere una regione simbolo," *Panorama*, October 28, 2010.
[7] Andrea Acquarone, "Timbravano il cartellino all'Asl poi lavoravano in centri privati – Arrestati 24 fra medici, infermieri, e tecnici. A inchiodarli le registrazioni di telecamere," in *Il Giornale*, November 16, 2010.

Sometimes a recommendation can be a bad thing. In Bologna,[8] a work contract, which was practically signed with Ignazio Marino, was torn up when he decided to run for the position of secretary to the *Pd* (Italian Democratic Party) against Pierluigi Bersani. In the Emilia-Romagna region, Bersani is the irrefutable leader.

The investigation conducted by a Parliamentary committee and presided by a deputy from Palermo, Leoluca Orlando,[9] concluded its research by presenting the dramatic numbers behind a small failure. Of 326 declared episodes of medical malpractice, 70 occurred in Calabria, 63 in Sicily, 32 in Lazio, and 23 in Puglia. This equates to one third of the population dealing with two thirds of the damage. But why?

Certain research groups maintain that the healthcare system wastes 9 billion Euro each year. This money is lost in unclear budget spending, unused operating rooms, and in pointless and expensive employment. This study was conducted by AIOP (Italian Association for Private Hospitalization).[10] They analyzed refunds obtained and compared them with the actual value of the service given. This method seems honest even though it is a biased party, and therefore could be accused of offering a one-sided opinion. In any case, when even the research is reprehensible due to some errors, the numbers cannot be called into question and overall the evaluations remain valid.

The Lazio region, which already had a debt of nine billion Euro that it accumulated between 2003 and 2008, added another significant debt.

---

[8] Mario Gerevini, "Porte chiuse all'anti Bersani. La Procura apre un'indagine," *Il Resto del Carlino*, December 27, 2010 and "Marino e la nomina di Bologna saltata per le primarie. AL telefono due medici raccontano: si è schierato da un'altra parte e gli hanno fatto il voltafaccia," *Il Resto del Carlino*, December 28, 2010.

[9] Filippo Maria Cutrupi, "Malasanità, in Calabria il record della vergogna. I dati drammatici della commissione parlamentare d'inchiesta: su 326 episodi di errori sanitari sull'intero territorio nazionale, 78 si sono verificati nella regione del Sud," *Il Giornale*, January 4, 2011.

[10] Nadio Delai, *Rapporto sanità*, Roma 2010. The results of the investigation were made public in a press conference by AIOP's National President, Enzo Paolini, the Vice-President, Gabriele Pellissero, and by Confindustria's General Manager, Giampiero Galli.

In Calabria, there were no records prior to 2009, when an administrative "hole" of one billion and a half Euro was signaled. There are 36 hospitals in that region. The one located in the town of Palmi has a budget of 13 million Euro and spends 10 million for the salaries of its personnel. The hospital in Cosenza cost around 49 million Euro and records show that it performs 100,000 operations per year, but 60% of those are classified as code white operations, and could be resolved with the assistance of the family's medical practitioner and does not require a trip to the emergency room. In Gioia Tauro, 26 chefs were hired for a hospital that had 32 beds, but the preparation of the meals was subcontracted to an external company. In Vibo Valentia, for 200 patients there are 115 doctors, 220 nurses, 16 assistants and 10 laboratory technicians.

In Campania, the debts have reached such absurd levels that it is necessary to spend 200 million Euro for lawyers to stave off the creditors.

According to researchers, a more careful management of the resources and more care taken in the services provided would allow Lazio to save two billion Euro (and change!), Calabria to save one billion and a half Euro, and Campania to save 3 billion Euro.

Let it be understood that the North also has some improvements to make. Lombardy could reduce its expenses by 874 million Euro and the Veneto region could reduce them by 697,000. Amongst the so-called "virtuous" regions, Piedmont is the one that is worse off. In the healthcare sector the expenses account for 82% of the budget. The comptroller-general released a study stating that in the last two years, the Leftist administration of Mercedes Basso accounted for the increase in debt from 7.9 to 8.2 billion Euro. What is happening? Putting aside substantial criminal behavior for the moment, efficiency is often left in the background. Politicians seem to believe that the healthcare system owes more to itself than to the citizens. It is a hierarchy of power and represents the opportunity to employ friends, supporters, those that are absolutely "necessary," and those to whom a favor is owed or from whom a favor is needed.

In Piedmont, there are 23 operational units that deal exclusively with hemodynamics when only 17 are absolutely necessary. Three of these are practically closed and 5 or 6 are infrequently used. How much does it cost the taxpayers to keep them all open anyway? A few billion Euro per year. This is only one example in an attempt to illustrate that a vast reorganization is necessary. In Piedmont, the objective is to ensure that the hospitals function as a network all while continuing to perform their regular services but without offering unnecessary duplicates. They should all reach an agreement.... Yet the powers of preservation demonstrate a certain staying power. The barons and local "bosses" raise their voices and sometimes manage to get in the way of reforms that are absolutely necessary.

The bigger picture regarding our institutions is a desolate one and would justify the speedy introduction of federalism.

We no longer have a goose that lays golden eggs and we are now running out of time.

There are 3,571,379 people that work in the public administration in Italy. In America, whose population is four times as numerous, there are half as many employees.

In the North there are 2.5 government employees for every one thousand citizens. In the Center, including Rome, there are 8.3 In the South, there are 9.2

This means that every resident in the Padania Valley in the North pays taxes that are 2.5 times higher in order to cover the cost of their own bureaucracy and that of the South. Why?

Sicily holds the record: there is 9 times the amount of government employees than in Lombardy: 27,000 versus 3,000

According to the statistics, there is a government employee for every 348 residents. In reality, there are actually three for every 348 residents. On the payroll of the towns, there are 28,000 forest rangers, 10,000 suppliers, and 22,500 employees without a fixed contract. They cannot be fired because they need 10 to 15 more years before they can retire. It is a disproportionate army of bureaucrats that, it would seem, are insufficient.[11] The region of Sicily published a call for bids to hire another 4,000 people. Half of those would be former employees without a long-term contract,[12] who would be granted one, and others who would be determined by an open competition that would be defined in 2011. It was only after it was declared as scandalous that the chapter on the employees with no long-term contracts was frozen.

To do what exactly? In the study entitled *Il burocrate di fronte alla burocrazia* (*The Bureaucrats Face the Bureaucracy*), an anonymous government official confesses and, at the same time, accuses: "In Sicily there are 80 vehicles that are used exclusively to chauffeur the maids of the regional councilors."[13]

Who is paying for all of this? How much is the North spending to keep its offices teeming with personnel?

According to the Cgia of Mestre (Association of Small Businesses and Artisans), each resident of the region of Lombardy pays 3000 Euro. Those in the Veneto region pay 1,000 Euro, those in Piedmont pay 150 Euro and those in Emilia Romagna pay 736 Euro. These are approximations.

Many years ago, the *Lega* political party from the North posted advertisements with "a goose that lays golden eggs." Those who were politically correct turned their noses up at this advertisement and considered Bossi to be insane. Today, we can better comprehend who effectively is insane. The truth of the matter is that the era of the "golden eggs" is over and shortly the goose will stop laying eggs altogether. Alessandro Vitale wrote in his dissertation on political parasitism:[14] "Plundering often does not encounter sufficient resistance on the part of the plundered." The consequences

---

[11] Vittorio Macioce, "La Sicilia balla sul Titanic – Nuovo persoale negli ospedali … a spese del resto d'Italia," *Il Giornale*, December 29, 2010.
[12] "E dopo lo scandalo, Lombardo fa dietrofront. Congelati gli stagisti," *Il Giornale*, January 8, 2011
[13] Gloria Pirzio Ammassari, Franco Ferraresi, and Federico Dell'Orto Farzonio, *Il burocrate di fronte alla burocrazia*, Rome, 1969.
[14] Alessandro Vitale, "Il parassitismo politico. La faccia nascosta dello stato moderno, impresa interna e internazionale di potere": lecture delivered at Turin's *Centro Congressi Unione Industriale* on March 25, 2009.

are still dramatic: "What often winds up bringing this cycle to a close is the destruction of wealth that results and that can provoke the breaking apart of the country."

This issue is so old that it appears to be ancient but let us turn the page.

In 1901, Giuseppe Zanardelli, a major figure in the Ten Day Revolt in Brescia, was a patriot who was exiled and then made a deputy, then a minister, and finally the Prime Minister. He took the opportunity to speak in Parliament and announced that the South's economy was getting progressively worse.

His prose was very direct, with no frills or rhetoric and for these reasons it was effective. He announced that, starting in 1861, the liberation of the South should not be the most important issue on the elite class of the North's agenda. Anytime economic and financial initiatives put the South at odds with the North, the North was always given the benefits.

Thunderous applause broke out from everyone,[15] but the decisions that were made did not seem sufficient to solve the grave issues at hand. They chose to "transform" the Basilicata region, promote the Industrial Revolution in Naples, and to build an aqueduct in Puglia.

This all remained exclusively on paper. Gaetano Salvemini was obliged to admit that the Puglian aqueduct had "fed" more people than quenched their thirst.[16] He was convinced that a dual morality existed in Italy. In the North, the more reactionary and mob-run government would not have taken the liberties that the more honest, liberal, and enlightened government of the South did. The public seemed to accept this state of affairs and, as though it were an ancient custom, was willing to be subjected to it.

More radical solutions were necessary. Luigi Einaudi tried to point the way in an article that was aptly entitled *"Via i prefetti"* (Let us do away with the prefects).[17] He demonstrated that the

---

[15] *Atti Parlamentari*, Rome 1900-1902.
[16] Gaetano Salvemini, in *Critica Sociale*, April 1, 1897.
[17] Luigi Einaudi, *Prediche inutili*, Turin 1956.

Unification of a country was not determined by the prefects, local superintendents of education, financial officers, town clerks, and the memorandums, instructions, and authorizations issued by Rome. He exclaimed, "The Unification is determined by the Italians ... who have learned at their own expense what it means to govern oneself."

To put it more briefly: that federalism tried to make its way through the forest of corporative interests.

The new constitution, though it called for the establishment of Regions, only rendered them effective thirty years later and with inadequate instruments.

In an essay of a rare caliber, Romano Bracalini[18] reconstructs step by step the complex relationship between the North and the South that evolved from a dialectical one to one of conflict.

After the elections of 1948, only men from the North held the most important positions in the State: Luigi Einaudi from Piedmont became President; Alcide de Gasperi from Trento became Prime Minister; Ivanoe Bonomi from Mantua became President of the Senate; Giovanni Gronchi from Pisa became President of the House of Deputies. To counterbalance this, the Neapolitan lawyer Giovanni Porzio was given a ministry without funds. So the South now had its advocate.

The work that had been interrupted (did it ever really begin?) could now resume. This included primarily the renewal of lands that had been destroyed and the growth of an agricultural system. Truly, the primary objective was to assign jobs rather than actually ensure that jobs were created.

To the North, this appeared wasteful. To the South this appeared to be adequate compensation. It was the price Italy had to pay for annexing the South. If up until that point the regions in the North sucked the lifeblood out of the South, from that moment onward, it became the South that took advantage of the North, without offering anything in return.

---

[18] Romano Bracalini, *Brandelli d'Italia,* Soveria Manelli 2010.

De Gasperi envisioned a development plan for the South that allotted 3 trillion Lira at the time, to be distributed over the course of thirty years.

That fund was to finance aqueducts, power plants, factories, irrigation systems, homes, schools, roads, and hospitals. All of that money was to help the businesses of the South to get off the ground.

It was all a wasted effort. In any liberal democracy it is not the State who promotes industry. The State builds the infrastructures that foster its growth and implements the laws that do so as well. In the North, the most successful industries were private. In the South they were built and directly run by the State. These industries were capable of crushing the private sector and therefore create a false economy.

The government decided to establish a fund for extraordinary works that would benefit the public, specifically for the South. The word "fund" troubled Piero Campili because he believed that it evoked notions of speculation and customers. De Gasperi liked the term used because he felt it evoked a sense of reassurance and that it gave the impression of an institution that "paid". They needed to give everyone the impression that this time they were serious and that things would get done.

The director of the Bank of Italy, Donato Menichella, went on the record as stating: "Let us pray to God that these funds truly reach their destinations without being rerouted!" The funds never arrived!

The one trillion Lira that were initially allotted, and issued by the Bank of Italy, became 9 trillion Lira from 1961 to 1971. Another 7.4 trillion Lira were allotted on October 6, 1972, which brought the total amount allotted to 16.4 trillion lira.

What an abundance for an army of students, consultants, managers, Pro-South activists, brokers, project designers, employees, bailiffs.... This fund met all the needs of those who managed it, who were clearly not managing their own money, and were therefore willing to meet even the most bizarre requests.

The money went towards financing businesses that did not exist and acted to boost the welfare system of the State, including naval shipyards located in the mountains and money laundering companies that produced nothing.

In 1962, Ugo La Malfa, the Minster of the Economy under the center-left administration of Amintore Fanfani, allotted the resources (which were to be obtained through more taxes) for a second "package."

It was the era of the "cathedral in the desert": factories that produced little or nothing and whose only objective was to assign titles for non-existent jobs. All they had to do was have their time card stamped.

We are speaking about 140 trillion Lira[19] worth of businesses that were dead before they were even born because they were created with no economic sense.

The better part of these businesses was completely imaginary. The French newspaper *Le Monde* counted the number of public projects that were undertaken but never completed. They numbered 380 and 160 of them were located in Sicily alone.

Foundries in Taranto; brickyards in Ragusa; the dam built on Mount Cotugno and completed in 1982 but never used; the airport in Potenza where snow is the true boss for many months of the year; the gigantic seaport in Sibari that was covered in sand as soon as the dredging machines finished their job: all of these were financed projects that were either never completed or never rendered functional.

When the Berlin Wall fell, West Germany literally bought East Germany and invested a mountain of money while betting on the future of Germany. In Bonn and Berlin there was no talk of *Risorgimento* or of resistance. They merely put their hands on their wallets.

If we had done the same thing it would have cost us far less. The Fathers of our Country could have directly bought the Southern provinces and the balance would have closed with minor liabilities.

---

[19] Pierluigi Ciocca and Gianni Toniolo, *Storia economica d'Italia*, Bari 1999.

The industries of the North paid to go South. The Alfa Sud car factories and those of Pomigliano are the result of a direct financing from the State. The State practically funded facilities, structures, and workers with tax money without stopping to consider how much they would cost and how much they actually produced.

The crisis that Fiat has faced in the past few months stems from this. In the past, the management and the workers had no interest in producing because the efficiency and productivity of the factories was not their primary objective. Now, the head offices have decided that the annual balance must break even, at the very least. They ask that sacrifices be made in proportion to those who want to continue to work and the right way to do this comprises applying agreements with the Unions that are based on their needs. Even when Bossi mentioned this and supported the need to enforce diversified contracts he was considered destructive. Even then, he had seen what was the right thing to do, and in advance.

Could Sergio Marchionne's decision to abandon national contracts constitute a refusal of (Union) centralism? Wouldn't leaving their hands freer to autonomously build and plan allow them to embark upon the road to (economic) federalism?

Society often runs faster than politics, and if politics does not keep up with it, it will find itself too far behind and inadequate to handle further problems.

CHAPTER 3

"Vienna is a thief…!" So is Naples

In the first half of the 1800s, Italy seemed quite similar to Europe a few years ago. It was a puzzle with frustratingly jagged borders.

A trip consisting of a few hundred kilometers – say from Turin to Bonn – was an obstacle course that one could only overcome by carrying the branch office of a sort of bank. As soon as one crossed the border, even only for a cup of coffee or for some gas, Swiss Francs were necessary. The French Francs were required in France. Just a little farther away, one needed Austrian Schillings, German Marks, and the individual currencies of Holland, Belgium and Luxembourg. The British Pound has always been powerful in terms of buying power and unfavorable to us.

Often, one wound up using dollars, whose value was immediately perceived and recognized by all, even though one would be left with change in coins from the various stops along the way.

It was the markets that called for a simplification of things in order to speed up commerce, exchanges, and trafficking. The introduction of the Euro was viewed as an economic necessity, even if Italy wound up accepting a very unfavorable exchange.

The Europe of the Banks had been created. There is nothing political about this at all. In fact, in Brussels and Strasbourg, politics is absent: entirely, as far as foreign problems are concerned and it is uncertain regarding other issues.

An example? When the Middle East Crisis broke out, Great Britain took the side of the United States against Saddam Hussein's Iraq. Aznar's Spain declared itself to be a "country at war but without being combative" while Zapatero, who had won the elections in the meantime, retreated from the conflict entirely. Italy participated to the post-war efforts on a peacekeeping mission.

The "European Commission for External Action" (which basically is a sort of Ministry of Foreign Affairs that operates from Brussels) was assigned to Catherine Ashton, who boasts the title of baroness. The activities conducted by this commission are actually a duplicate of the initiatives that each single state develops on their own. The rest is quite simply a display of embassies in every corner of the world, even in those countries where, frankly, diplomacy appears to be quite superfluous.

Why are 35 people assigned to the Fiji Islands? Why are there 23 in Papua New Guinea? Do we really need headquarters in Tonga, Samoa, and the Solomon Islands?

To host such a headquarters, a building needed to be rented for the sum of 12 million Euro per year. The best part is that not everyone fits. The twenty diplomats that represent Europe in Brussels need another small building next to this one, for practical purposes, but separate in order to respect the professionalism of which each is particularly jealous.

Are there any protests? Are there any scandals[1]? Disputes? Everything is covered up. Everyone pretends not to see and not to hear.

When one speaks of Europe, one speaks of a taboo subject. It just so happens that an extremely important treaty, like that drawn in Lisbon, which calls from some significant changes for millions of citizens, is approved with practically no argument. The *Lega* party is constantly opposed because it often interjects with its opinion and often states uncomfortable truths.

This brings us to questions of money. At the first hint of problems that might involve the markets a "code red alarm" goes off and the defenders of the Euro emerge. "We must not hide the fact that there are troubling signs present at the moment. The single currency is in danger." Money, which is considered the "primary

---

[1] Gian Micalessin, "Il pozzo senza fondo delle ambasciate Ue – 136 sedi diplomatiche disseminate nel mondo anche in paesi esotici come Tonga – Sprecati tre miliardi di euro l'anno," *Il Giornale*, December 6, 2010.

spoil," is the esthetic element that guarantees the integration of the adhering states[2].

Even in Pre-Unification Italy, the geo-political climate denounced excessive division. This purportedly took into consideration that travel between cities was rare because it was arduous due to the many borders and customs taxes that had to be paid.[3]

The Duke governed Modena, but Piacenza was ruled by a Duchess and Florence had been assigned to the Grand Duke. Around all of those laid the Pontifical State. In the North, the Lombard and Veneto regions were ruled by the Savoys. In the South, there was the Kingdom of the Two SIciles.

Each little state had its own currency that was not even a close relative to its neighbor. Only the Kingdom of Sardinia used the decimal system so one had to take into consideration various multiples and submultiples of various consistencies. It was a patchwork of a country.

The business world, therefore, preferred to use the Turkish currency – the "dollar" of Europe's yesteryear – and the claims of speedier commerce were put forth as an excuse to reorganize the borders.

Talk about romanticized dreams of an ideologically unified Italy, which, though they did exist, did so only in the world of poets. The first projects that reorganized the country called for a customs "league" that would allow for travel without inconveniences regarding the payment of the duties for commercial products in circulation.

Even in this case, economic issues are handled before political ones.[4]

The plan was to construct a sort of federalism that would function like a Board of Directors, where each government would have a proportionate share. The position of President would be assigned to the Pope-King due to his moral suasion-vested authority

[2] Luigi Grassia, "Napolitan: a rischio la moneta unica – I mercati temono il contagio della crisi del debito ai paesi iberici," *La Stampa*, November 27, 2010.
[3] Romano Bracalini, *L'Italia prima dell'Unità (1815-1860)*, Milan 2001.
[4] Giovanni Ansaldo, *L'Italia com'era*, Naples 1992.

that all attributed to him. This would be equivalent to receiving the golden share.

The rest would have to remain untouched. Even though the states were small, they were very jealous of the system of institutions upon which they had been founded. They had traditions that, though they were entirely unknown to those even a few kilometers away, were deeply rooted in the collective imagination of their people. No one dreamed of decreasing the margins of their own freedom. Quite the contrary: they aimed to increase each of their autonomies.

The original, authentic inspiration for the *Risorgimento* was quite far from the concept of "Unification" that, unfortunately, took hold in Italy due to political short-sightedness and a series of unpredictable chance occurrences.

In 1848, the people of Milan gave rise to the Five Day Insurrection in order to rid themselves of the master they already had and not to choose another one.

To use more modern terms, the Lombards rebelled and shouted "Vienna is a thief!"[5] They did not understand why they had to send their tax money to Austria and wait for its return in order to carry out the projects they needed.

Truthfully, the Habsburg government did not steal[6]: it was efficient by definition. It did not waste its resources and their severe doctrines prevented them from infringing this notion, especially when the public sphere was concerned. One could not say that Lombardy and the Veneto region were poorly governed, but why not take care of oneself? The Austrians could worry about Austria and the Milanese could worry about Milan.

The various rebels harbored many different schools of thought. Each one was a military commander of themselves and a rabble-rouser for a political party that they forced themselves to personally and exclusively represent.

---

[5] Leone Tettoni, *Cronaca della rivoluzione di Milano*, Milan 1848.
[6] Romano Bracalini, *L'Italia prima dell'Unità (1815-1860)*, cit.

Amongst these rebels, Carlo Cattaneo managed to distinguish himself. He supported the theory of a "people's war" whose main objective was to transform Lombardy into an independent region.[7] This is why he chose to contribute his ideas and words to *Il Cisalpino*[8] newspaper and not *L'italiano*.

On the opposite side was Gabrio Casati, the Mayor of Milan. He held the highest political rank at the time and believed it was necessary to seek the help of Charles Albert of Savoy's army. It was the only army well organized enough to fight against the Austrians[9].

These different opinions turned into fighting and these fights turned into controversies, often violent ones. Nevertheless, no one, not even those who fervently placed the barricades in the center of the city and defended them, believed that their own hides were worth risking, only to become a slave of Rome, while passing through Turin.

Would anyone really cause a revolution just to change masters? It is worth noting that the Five Day Insurrection in Milan was the only episode of involvement on the part of the people in the entire history of the *Risorgimento*. The enthusiasm proceeded to dwindle and completely disappear because even the most enthusiastic rebels had to take note that the Savoys had no interest whatsoever in forming Italy but truly only wanted to continue their "artichoke"[10] politics,[11] adding territorial conquests for themselves while damaging their neighbors.

Certainly, the change of address, from Vienna to Turin, regarding where tax money would be sent, could neither be considered an improvement nor an objective. The alliance with the Savoy king was supposed to be a tactic to free them from foreign

---

[7] Romano Bracalini, *Cattaneo, un federalista per gli italiani*, Milan 1995.
[8] Giuseppe Armani, *Carlo Cattaneo, il padre del federalism italiano*, Milan 1997.
[9] Luigi Torelli, *Ricordi intorno alle Cinque Giornate di Milano*, Milan 1976.
[10] Massimo Viglione, *Identità ferit: il Risorgimento come rivoluzione e la Guerra civile italiana*, Milan 2006
[11] TRANSLATOR'S NOTE: To possess something piece by piece similar to the way in which one eats an artichoke, leaf by leaf.

rule and was not to be intended as a preamble to a new slavery that would become even more frustrating because it was sought.

After all, the Kingdom of Piedmont (back then) was not, and the Piedmont of today is not, a monolith.

What is the evidence of this? On November 9, 1850, in Turin, Margherita Trotti Bentivoglio made this comment:[12] "We speak of a United Italy, but this little state of ours consists of four provinces that share nothing in common. There is Sardinia, which is only half-civilized. Genoa nurtures the same feelings towards Piedmont that Lombardy felt towards Austria. In the Savoy kingdom one finds the other extreme: more than half of them are ultra-conservatives. Turin is the only healthy part of the kingdom".

Indirectly, this analysis found confirmation in the thoughts of Lorenzo Valerio in a letter he wrote in reply to one written by the Hungarian patriot Lajos Kossuth. In it, he imagined a series of political scenarios that were only beginning to take shape. "Genoa and all of the provinces on that side of the Sesia River will turn to Lombardy. The Savoy kingdom, Nice, Aosta, and Pinerolo will side with either France or Switzerland. Turin will be reduced to nothing."[13] There was great distrust in the region of Sardinia alone. In 1848, the only ones who wanted a united Italy were Genoa and Sardinia[14] but only to decrease the rigid control that Piedmont held over their respective regions.

Even in this third millennium it is not difficult to distinguish between three different sociological areas in Piedmont. Novara, Vercelli, and the Verbano-Cusio-Ossola area are still operating with an economy that was established during the Duchy of Milan. To the right of the Po River lies the land that belonged to the Savoy Kingdom. In the area surrounding the city of Alessandria,

---

[12] Adolfo Omode, *Conversazioni con uomini politicie personaggi eminent italiani*, Bari 1937. In the passage cited, the participants were Giacinto Provana of Collegno (a patriot of the failed revolution of 1821), his wife, the British economist Nassau William Senior, Fortunato Prandi (an exile from 1821) the Marquis Cesare Alfieri and the Marquis Gustavo di Cavour.

[13] Lajos Kossuth, *Carte*, National Archive in Budapest. The letter cited was written in French.

[14] Martin Clark, *Il Risorgimento italiano – Una storia ancora controversa*, Milan1998.

about a dozen or so square kilometers that include the town of Novi Ligure, the people share more affinity with the people of Genoa. Toponymy does not lie. The local dialect has a Ligurian cadence and the rod that is used to measure the fields also comes from that area as well.

Today, the major effort consists of strengthening Piedmont by establishing policies that bind the territories to one another. With a governor that is not influenced by Turin, this mission aims to create new prospects through the recognition of each area's role in the region. The province no longer means "minor league" in the hierarchy of attention. The square kilometer surrounding the most popular political circle no longer counts. If one strengthens the identity of the individual, the entire system reaps the benefits.

Hints of federalism were present already in the 1800s, before the Unification of Italy and, still today, federalism must be taken into consideration.

The challenges upon which Italy gambled its future were the need for administrative independence and the peaceful coexistence of so many groups of individuals.

Between 1848 and 1849, both Venice and Rome rebelled and declared the Republic.[15] This was not necessarily in opposition to a monarchy in particular, but rather served as a marker for the desire for independence that characterized the rebels.

In 1860 – in order to use an analogous "modern" simile – Palermo favorably greeted Garibaldi's *Mille* soldiers by shouting "Naples is a thief!" The Sicilians did not understand why their tax money was collected and sent to the Bourbon monarchs in Portici and that they had to await the money's return, either. Even if no money was lost during this trip (and money was certainly lost) it would have been in any case a waste of time and energy to go to and from the destinations in question when everything could be handled locally.

---

[15] Claudio Fracassi, *La meravigliosa storia della repubblica dei briganti*, Milan 2005.

On the island, the desire to do things themselves is rooted within their history.[16] Sicily rose from the colonization by the *siculi* and the *sicani* people who had learned to coexist but who nonetheless maintained their differences and, often, distances. Even the Bourbon monarchy could not overlook that outburst of independence and they agreed to give the governor of the island a full title. Francis and Ferdinand were not kings of Naples but of the Kingdom of the Two Sicilies and in Sicily they nominated a viceroy that had an enormous amount of power with respect to the other districts in the kingdom. This was to formally acknowledge the autonomy that the people claimed.

Little was done for the local people. The people asked for more radical reforms in order to ensure that they could govern themselves. But it is evident that the Sicilians did not want to rebel against Naples in order to subject themselves to Turin either.

Still today, they exhibit a great deal of local pride and they still believe that it is necessary to be the architects of their own future. Andrea Vecchio, President of the Builder's Association, in a speech given at the Cutuli Foundation stated: "We are like Afghanistan under the heel of the central government."[17]

Maurizio Zamparini, a man of the North as far as his roots are concerned, was rumored to have had close ties to the *Alleanza Nazionale* party (on the Right). He was also the owner of the Palermo soccer team. He declared that he was considering a foray in the political sphere. He did not intend to create a new political party but wanted to be an opinion leader. To do what? "I imagine a confederate Italy with strong areas like Sicily given a power similar to that given to the Swiss Cantons."[18]

Even the President of the Veneto Region, Raffaele Lombardo, made his opinion abundantly clear. He hypothesized the "seces-

---

[16] Mario Spataro, *I primi secessionist: separatismo in Sicilia1866 e 1943-46*, Naples 2001.
[17] *Atti del Convegno della Fondazione Cutuli*, Santa Venerina (Catania), November 19 2010.
[18] "Zamparini scende in campo: dal 4-4-2 al federalism," in *Il Giornale*, October 27 2010

sion" of his land. He maintained that "the Unification of Italy was not a good deal, at least nor for us Venetians."[19] It was a single blanket, that was too short and too tattered, that wound up trying to cover too many realities that were too different from one another and that forced them to give up the individuality of which they were proud.

Our true national "DNA" was formed during the time of city-states and kingdoms, when the main focus, and love, towards one's own borders represented the true fundamental characteristic of one's identity. It was the Renaissance that best characterized Italy, not the *Risorgimento*. It is not unusual to find that still today neighboring towns, even in the same region, share a mutual and cordial aversion towards one another. At one time, this meant war and alliances were forged with communities that were more distant in order to defeat those that were close by. Today, the vestiges of ancient jeers have re-emerged and there are cultural trenches that are difficult to mend.

"*I pisan veder Lucca non ponno*" (The citizens of Pisa cannot bear to look at the town of Lucca) is the esthetic metaphor for many aspects of a society that is constructed around its local church steeple.

"*Veneziani gran signori, padovani gran dottori, vicentini magna gatti, veronesi tutti matti.*" (The Venetians are gentlemen, those from Padua are great scholars, those from Vicenza eat cats, and those from Verona are entirely crazy.)

Each area of the country has established certain hierarchies and values that have become a sort of legacy and are to be taken in part seriously and in part with a sense of humor.

Whoever dealt with the project to transform Italy in such a way that it became different from what it was could not ignore the need for autonomy that each community expressed.

Even Giuseppe Mazzini (who was thin, pale, and perhaps even impotent) the idealist that was a revolutionary Churchgoer

---

[19] Stefano Lorenzetto, "Intervista a Raffaele Lombardo: "Ma quale Padania! Sta volta è il Sud che fa la secessione," *Il Giornale*, October 28 2010.

and whose image is that of the quintessential Pro-Unitarian, envisioned a State composed of "overlapping concentric circles". The circles represented the single areas of the country, each with its own wealth and diversity. He specified, "We Republicans believe that the various entities of the State, including the financial, judicial, and educational institutions need to reside in their respective places throughout Italy."[20]

Marco Minghetti commented, "How much grief would have been spared if Italy had settled on political, diplomatic, and military Unification and chose to respect the traditions of the individuals throughout the various regions...."[21]

Mingetti pronounced those words 145 years ago. On November 24, 2010, the sociologist Luca Ricolfi published a peremptory editorial: *Federalismo: è già troppo tardi*.(Federalism: It's already too late) His conclusion sends chills up one's spine: "If we wait until 2013[22] or 2014, then perhaps we will no longer have any businesses upon which we can apply these laws."

The most productive areas of the country are suffocated under the weight of the bureaucracy and the taxes. Every year, the North (Piedmont, Lombardy, and the Veneto region) writes a check of 50 billion Euro for the rest of Italy. These numbers are the results of a study conducted by the Confederation of Artisans from Mestre and they refer to 2007. According to this study, if one adds the region of Emilia-Romagna's contribution, the amount rises to 56 billion Euro.

This is too much. This too large of a commitment to make and it becomes unbearable in the light of the uncertain benefit the receivers would obtain. A disproportionate "bribe" does not respect the contributive capacity of the producer and risks to be inefficient if the beneficiary wastes it by dispersing it into thousands of useless rivulets. This is not a question of refusing to offer solidarity by calling upon egotistical motivations, but it is rather necessary

---

[20] Giuseppe Mazzini, *Lettere politiche*, Trani 1895.
[21] Marco Minghetti, *Scritti Vari*, Bologna 1896.
[22] Luca Ricolfi, "Federalismo: E' già troppo tardi," *La Stampa*, November 24 2010.

to create counterweights that would serve to keep the entire system in balance.

The reasons offered by the past are no longer adequate and are too few.

The historical schools of thought recognize that 150 years ago, the South was mistreated. It is not necessary to be a Neo-Bourbonist or lover of Southern Italy to see this. It is sufficient to clear the Romanticism from the *Risorgimento*, which was responsible for turning commonplace events into a story of epic proportions. The so-called wars of independence did not propose to export liberty but rather to conquer new provinces. Naples and Palermo were considered as Mogadishu and Addis Abeba were, more recently. The victors occupied the Kingdom of the Two Sicilies and considered those lands a colony to exploit. They sucked all of the resources and – out of rudeness, incompetence, carelessness, or laziness – allowed what they could not steal, to steadily decay. In this manner, they managed to destroy even vast fortunes.[23]

For the past few decades, however, the North and the South have exchanged roles. It is now the South that sucks away at the North's resources with the result being that the North cannot take it anymore.

In one hundred and fifty years empires live and die. In Europe, two world wars have been fought. Nazism imposed itself and then disappeared. The communism proposed by the Soviet Union knew great success and failure. Must the *Risorgimento* be the milestone with which other events measure themselves?

At the dawn of this third millennium, the South transformed itself into a ball and chain around the country's foot that no longer allows the leg to move freely. Centralism has developed a "Roman" system that survives by draining public resources. It is as though during these transactions that one seems to pay a sort of brokerage fee that appears to be much higher (proportionately) than the fee one pays to purchase property.

---

[23] Vincenzo Gulì, *Il saccheggio del Sud*, Naples 1998.

Stupid people can get away with saying "Who cares?" and at best can conjure up some ideological cover: "You wanted us. Now you can keep us." A pinch of reason is all that is necessary to understand that the failure of a country should concern everyone: those that could have prospered, those who would have been happy to carry on, and those who with lots of effort could have survived. If everyone goes under, it is pointless to conjure up centuries-old justifications.

We must make peace with the past so that we do not compromise our present.

Therefore, if the taxes were reduced to 40 billion Euro (30 billion would be even better) it would allow the stronger regions to get back on their feet and to be more prepared to face the competition that other, more industrialized states pose. It would allow these regions to enter the market with quality products.

Without corrective measures, even the most industrialized and productive parts of the country will be unable to handle the weight of such oppressive taxation.

Even if one has good legs with which to run, they would be forced to kneel if faced with a broken back. On the contrary, the benefits stemming from an increase in competitiveness would not only benefit the protagonists of the development, but would rain upon the South as well.

CHAPTER 4

Two "World" Wars and a Truckload of Lies

Count Camillo Benso of Cavour's thoughts about Italy's future ran the gamut. He was a swindling genius and, behind his tiny spectacles for his shortsightedness, managed to see quite far into the future before many others did. He was wider than he was tall and had a rather large belly that did not prevent him from giving up his five course lunches. He was a gifted man but because of his gifts he felt encouraged to abuse his intelligence and cleverness.

He was an enormous liar. Once his trickery had been unveiled, he was no longer taken seriously throughout Europe: "the one thing that you would believe to be truly impossible was exactly what he was asserting."[1]

A posthumous examination of Cavour's intentions is as muddy as the study of patristic philosophy. In public and private conversations, semi-public and semi-private conversations, he made every effort to please his conversation partners in order to obtain some advantage or at the very least to eliminate the nuisances derived from dissent. Everyone, even those who started off being in direct opposition to him, wound up convincing themselves they were all on the same wavelength.[2]

It is possible to apply numerous shades to any color scheme. Nonetheless, even with considerable reservations, it was a widely held opinion that Cavour spoke of a Piedmontese nation and of a Sicilian one that were distant and distinct from one another. They each had characteristics and peculiarities that needed to be pre-

---

[1] Massimo D'Azeglio, *Lettere al fratello Roberto*, Milan 1872.
[2] Annabella Cabiati, *Cavour: fece l'Italia, visse con ragione, amò con passione*, Villorba (Treviso) 2010.

served. His concept of "Italianicity" did not go beyond the regions of the North, which shaped the kingdom of Napoleon Bonaparte. There is little evidence that shows he desired visiting any part of Italy that was outside the borders of Piedmont. He never even saw Sardinia which was part of the Savoy kingdom. He worked very hard to speak Italian well, but he was more at ease when he spoke French and he also conversed well in English. He was quite familiar with the history and politics of those countries that were north of the Alps and did not care for that of his own country.[3]

In 1851, Vincenzo Gioberti published *Rinnovamento civile degli italiani* (The Renewal of the Italian Civilization). In this text, he wrote in praise of Count Camillo Benso stating that "he was a man of talent" however, "unfortunately, he held very little interest for issues pertaining to Italy."

Cavour envisioned a larger Piedmont and not an Italy in which one drowned one's identity. From 1862, a few months after his death, the Republicans and Democrats whispered that if it had been up to Cavour "the boot would have had no heel."[4]

From the beginning, his government initiative aimed to move the geopolitical borders so that Victor Emanuel II could comply with his own dynastic ambitions (and those of his forefathers): acquiring the Veneto region and Lombardy. To Cavour, the Unification of Italy with the centralization of its institutions, which eventually happened, was "utter nonsense"[5] that he believed could be averted.

In the mayhem that ensued concerning the conquest of Rome, he stated that it would be nice to "have a capital for celebrations and one for work." Finally, he stated "I am neither certain that we will be able to enter Rome nor if that would be desirable." If we had to go down that road, "it would have been to celebrate our triumph, but not to stay there."[6]

---

[3] Denis Mack Smith, *Cavour, il grande tessitore dell'unità d'Italia*, Milan 1985.
[4] Mario Costa Cardol, *Ingovernabili da Torino: i tormentati esordi dell'unità d'Italia*, Milan 1989.
[5] *Ibidem.*
[6] William de La Rive, *Vita di Cavour*, Milan 1961.

Keep in mind that Cavour comes off as being the "weaver" of the fabric of the Italian State as though his design was clear from the beginning and that the path undertaken had been planned down to the last detail. This is clearly an exaggeration. Some aspects were determined by chance, others by luck, still others simply went in a given direction and that was that.

Certainly Count Camillo Benso was able to carry a project to term that few were willing to believe possible. He did so with lucidity and pragmatism. In order to reach his objective, he unleashed two conflicts that could be considered of global importance at the time. He inebriated half of Europe with his chatter. He looked no one in the face and resorted to using dirty trickery to avoid obstacles and to turn them into advantages. It was evident from the very beginning that in that tiny, ungraceful body, while there was room for roasted pheasant, jugged hare, and boiled meat in green sauce, there was no room for any scruples.

The first move in this complicated game of chess was to participate in the Crimean War. Russia and Turkey were fighting to control a few dozen square kilometers of a peninsula in the Black Sea. Initially, this conflicted presented itself as one of the many contentious incidents in that region. The Catholics and the Orthodox Christians were fighting to gain control of the locations that were sacred to all Christians in the area. At other times, often, the squabbles were quelled with a solution that, even if it did not please everyone, gave both sides a reason to put their rifles down.

In 1854, the fighting escalated to such a point that it turned into a clash of global proportions that sent the world's diplomacy into a state of disarray. Historians have reflected upon the conflict's causes for a very long time and have concluded that there are no evident causes and no reasons that are sufficient to explain why the conflict spread to such an extent.[7] France and England sided with Turkey while the Balkans aided Russia. Initially, it seemed that Austria would choose to side with the czar but then chose to side with the Western Block.

---

[7] Robert Edgerson, *Gloria o morte*, Milan 1999.

What about Piedmont? Cavour decided to participate in the war. "Decided to participate" should be taken quite literally because he offered the assistance of the army without consulting with the Council of Ministers, when it was widely known that the majority of the Ministers were against any participation. His politics, including his foreign policies, were elaborated without consideration for his colleagues. In fact, he did not even collaborate with the Minister of Foreign Affairs.

In this circumstance, there were many contrasting opinions because any gains seemed remotely impossible to attain. The few possibilities that were present were difficult to calculate and impossible to explain. The Minister of Foreign Affairs, the count and general, Giuseppe Dabormida, felt as though his authority had been undermined and felt that this action was one of distrust in his abilities. He submitted his resignation, which was promptly accepted.

Cavour relied on all of his dialectical abilities to support the notion that an international victory was indispensable in demonstrating the value of the Piedmontese army. A war against Russia would have made Piedmont appear as a champion of liberty. This argument was as weak as the military contingency that was sent on the mission.

In April of 1855, General Alfonso La Marmora left Genoa commanding 15,000 marksmen for Balaclava. They left with a large handicap, however. When the ships lifted their anchors in the Bay of San Fruttuoso, a fire broke out on the hospital ship and all of the medical supplies were lost. The troops left with no medicines and supplies. They also left without any specific order to do so. The commander did not know if his moves were to be autonomous or if he had to collaborate with someone. He did not know if he should report to the British or the French. His orders were generic: use your common sense. Usually this is good advice; however, sometimes it is not enough.

Upon returning home with the remaining troops, La Marmora confessed that had he known the embarrassment that this ambiguous condition would have brought about, he would have resigned before leaving.

The Crimean War was the triumph of tragedy and inefficiency.

The "Western" fleet bombed Kamc akta, but the result was so disappointing that the admiral committed suicide out of shame[8].

In Inkerman, twelve thousand Russians died along with four thousand Englishmen and Frenchmen.

The winter was ruthless. The wind destroyed twenty-six ships and diseases decimated the troops. The soldiers did not have the correct equipment and their clothes were too light for the frigid temperatures they had to face. Even in their tents, men lost fingers and toes from the cold. They died of gangrene and begged their fellow soldiers to put them out of their misery so that they would not have to suffer any longer. Typhoid fever destroyed the French troops. Cholera destroyed the Piedmontese marksmen.[9]

There were no battles, leaving little room for victory. The most famous incident that emerged from this war was the British assault to the Russian artillery in Balaclava.[10] It would be remembered as a heroic episode thanks to the poem that Tennyson wrote and the movie that the Americans made. From a military standpoint, the action was terribly disorganized. In fact, the entire attack was the result of a misunderstanding that was attributed to Captain Raglan, an official of little value who would only be remembered historically for the male fashion trend he set by having his coats tailor-made.

The Piedmontese marksmen only fought on the Chernaya River and proceeded to interrupt the path taken by Russian soldiers. Fourteen soldiers died and the clash was most likely nothing worthy of note except for the fact that it gave Turin bragging rights on an international scale. It was not nearly as important as the Napoleonic victory in Austerlitz.

---

[8] Camille Rousset, *Histoire de la guerre de Crimee, Paris 1894*.
[9] Aristide Calani, *Scene della vita militare in Crimea*, Naples 1855.
[10] Cecil Woodham-Smith, *Balaclava, la carica dei 600*, Milan 2002.

Piedmont paid for this undertaking with 1500 casualties. Cavour climbed up onto the mountain of corpses and claimed the right to participate to the peace conference, which was to be held in Paris to settle the remaining matters.

Certainly he would have preferred the war to have lasted longer and to have had more casualties. The more sacrifices Piedmont had made, the more merit and expectations it would have had the right to claim.

As things stood, it would be difficult to ask for significant compensation for war damages.

The conference was held on February 25, 1856. The delegations were welcomed in the new headquarters of the Ministry of Foreign Affairs on the Quai d'Orsay.

Karl Ferdinand von Buol-Schauenstein represented Austria, Lord Clarendon represented England, Vincent Benedetti represented France, Baron Manteuffel represented Prussia, Count Alexei Orloff represented Russia and Alì Pascià represented Turkey. Piedmont had acquired a seat of international importance and immediately laid claim to another seat as well: one for Count Cavour and the other for Salvatore Pes of Villamarina.

The conference was presided over by Count Floryan Walewski, the Minister of Foreign Affairs of France.[11] On the main table, suspended by a solid gold support, was an eagle quill pen that was waiting to be used by the delegates to sign the final document of approval.

The protagonists of the conference were faced with an arduous task at the negotiation table. Truth be told, it actually consisted of a number of "tables" and once they were set, they remained so well into the night. Damremont confessed, "We try to treat our guests well but what is most surprising is the resistance put up by our guests in the battle of forks and knives."[12] The dinner table is the ideal place to forge new diplomatic friendships and to draw

---

[11] Franz Herre, *Napoleone III*, Milan 1994.
[12] Arrigo Petacco, *L'amante imperial: amori, intrighi e segreti della contessa di Castiglione*, Milan 2000.

up solutions because it establishes an informal setting. In this manner, one speaks more freely and propositions appear less arduous to defend and less embarrassing to refuse.

What about Cavour? "The count," commented Walewski, "appears to be quite moderate in his interventions during the discussions. However, in the corridors he moves around too much, conspires with the delegates, and gives tendentious interviews." Cavour himself admitted that he "writhed to and fro like the Devil in holy water." He wrote to Emanuele D'Azeglio, "I try to be friendly towards everyone, even with the ladies and their dogs. My success lies in the fact that they ruined one of my new outfits."[13]

What about the results? There were few at first. Piedmont was actually excluded from the preliminary summit and the delegates did not seem willing to listen what this small area at the foot of the Alps had to say.

Count Camillo Benso behaved like a busybody, like always. He arranged to have Paris and London each receive mutually contradictory messages, stating that they had found in him a faithful ally. He also tried to win over the defeated though it was uncertain how they would be able to help him in any way. To corrupt the Russian delegates, he brought with him an enormous amount of cash that he took from the funds of the secret service,[14] which he spent right down to the last cent. The accounting books were manipulated in such a manner that all of the expenses appeared to be legitimate.

Cavour became the spokesperson of some truly fantastic propositions. He wanted Lombardy back from Austria and proposed that Austria be allowed to annex the principalities of Wallachia and Moldavia in exchange. He also suggested that a marriage of interest be arranged between the Prince of Carignano, a cousin of Victor Emanuel II, and the Duchess of Parma. The newlyweds would then be sent off to Moldavia, where they would be crowned

---

[13] Camillo Benso Conte di Cavour (curated by Rosario Romeo), *Scritti inediti e rari*, Santena (Turin) 1971.
[14] Denis Mack Smith, *Cavour il grande tessitore dell'unità d'Italia*, cit.

king and queen. To justify this initiative, besides the political benefits, was the certainty that this member of the Savoy family "would have revitalized the Romanian race." Or perhaps it would have been better to continue pondering a royal wedding, but rather than sending the couple to Moldavia, Greece would have been a more suitable location.

In the end, Piedmont's compensation was reduced to allowing Cavour to give a speech regarding the Italian situation. This occurred on April 8, 1856. While no formal decisions were made, both the English and French delegates expressed their disapproval for the government of Naples and requested that there be structural changes made in the Southern Italian states. Vienna felt as though it had just received a slap in the face. With everyone in agreement, it appeared as though they were preparing for a trial in which Austria would play the role of the accused. "A placatory measure...."[15] Clarendon tried to minimize the importance of this occurrence in order to calm the Hapsburgs down. The Austrian envoys reacted and in some instances were actually able to obtain a few points in their favor. History is often called to forget unfavorable details, but the Austrian delegate defended himself by accusing Piedmont of being what it actually was: an illiberal country that arbitrarily presided over an independent state. Effectively, with the upheavals in 1848, troops from Turin had occupied the Principality of Monaco, which despite being physically surrounded by Piedmont had held the title of sovereign state up until that point. The controversy that ensued comprised a series of petulantly assiduous complaints on the part of the dethroned Prince Florestan of Monaco towards the world's governments requesting that they re-establish his right. France and England were repeatedly requested to act as mediators. It was only a modest occupation, but it was an occupation nonetheless. From what pulpit would it be possible to contest the Austrian occupation in Italy when the Italians themselves were guilty of the same act on their own territory?

---

[15] Adriano Viarengo, *Cavour*, Rome 2010.

Cavour already had problems dealing with all the criticism he received from both sides of the Parliament. Brofferio, on the left, complained that the country was brought into war on the basis of false promises. Solaro della Margherita, on the right, stated that while the army had fought with honor, an inept diplomatic delegation was unable to do its job in Paris. Amongst the "civilized" members of high society there were only weak complaints, but their disappointment was evident.

Count Camillo Benso attempted to quell the wave of disfavor that inundated him by disclosing a series of "facts" that were intended to justify his interventions. He stated that Clarendon was "impatient" to draw Great Britain in a war "to enlarge Piedmont." It was not exactly believable at that time either. When Cavour died, his memoirs and papers were published including those documents that spoke about this matter concerning Great Britain. Clarendon took great pains to formally refute this information stating that this was all "Impossible. A statement of this type is in direct contrast to the very principles of British politics."[16]

The Cavour of this time period was "completely insane" trying to keep after his "Italian schemes" and had "no scruples regarding the means he used to attain his goals."

He committed another political blunder. In London, he convinced the opposition, the conservative Tories, to put pressure on their government and offered them a reason to begin a parliamentary debate. He believed that he had the ability to manipulate the prime minister into openly supporting his project to redesign the boundaries inside of Italy. He obtained both insult and injury for himself. When his plotting was unveiled he was forced to admit his guilt and had to apologize using the justification that he was not familiar with the British parliamentary style (which was highly unlikely). The issue was closed in London and they continued to show their support of Piedmont but hinted that they would no longer trust Cavour. His possible ally risked to become a potential adversary.

---

[16] Denis Mack Smith, *Cavour, il grande tessitore dell'unita` d'Italia*, cit.

However, looking back, the first stone was placed in the foundation of the structure that Cavour intended to build.

A stone is necessary to start an undertaking. What about afterward?

The second stone in Cavour's structure consisted of a pair of sea green silk pajamas that looked quite stunning draped over the shoulders of Virginia Oldoini Rapallini. She was the wife of the Count of Castiglione and the lover of an infinite amount of very influential people.

Her friends called her "*Nicchia*" (the "Niche") and she was a splendid specimen of womankind. She was beautiful, likeable, and elegant. She was very refined in her gestures and with her sophisticated knowledge of culture she naturally found the doors of high society open. She took full advantage of this opportunity.

CHAPTER 5

Underwear Diplomacy and Encrypted Messages

In order to convince Napoleon III to intervene against Austria, *Nicchia*'s "public relations" were far more effective than any diplomatic measure. She even offered the use of her bedroom to settle the matter. Her objective with the French emperor was to ensure that the Savoy family would become the monarchs of Italy. "You must succeed, dear cousin," said Cavour, offering his blessing, "use whatever means you need, but succeed!"[1] Cavour wrote in a message to the Minister of Foreign Affairs, "I am warning you that I have recruited the beautiful Countess of Castiglione to join the ranks of the Piedmontese diplomacy. I have invited her to seduce the emperor.... I have requested for her father to be assigned the position of embassy secretary in St. Petersburg." Mission accomplished!

She was the most fascinating woman of the 1800s and knew that she could count on her talent as a *chanteuse* and was not ashamed to do so. She needed to deceive Napoleon III in the political sphere, flirt with him and, if necessary, seduce him. She managed to get straight to the heart of the matter: she seduced him and embarked on a patriotic love affair in which bed sheets and State matters were so intertwined that they appeared to be one and the same thing.

Nicchia had had many lovers in her lifetime, beginning when she was about eleven years old. Sometimes she had to juggle two or three boyfriends at a time. The most difficult task involved coordinating their visits so as not to risk their crossing paths on her doorstep as they entered and exited her home. She considered the affair with the emperor of France as a sort of final exam for her

---

[1] Marcus De Rubris, *Confidenze di Massimo D'Azeglio*, Milan 1930.

"degree" that would, however, leave her, at least from an exclusively erotic viewpoint, quite disappointed. When the lights go out, even the most powerful show their true colors.

Their first encounter occurred in Compiègne.[2] She looked as wonderful as usual and wore a dress that pushed her chest higher and left her back bare. She had been invited to attend the inauguration of a carousel with wooden horses which could only be built at that time in the park of the royal palace.

It must have been quite a spectacle to see those sculptures chase each other to the rhythm of music. Perhaps they spun too fast and when the carousel stopped, *Nicchia*'s head continued to spin. Napoleon III seized the opportunity and ran to her aid: "Perhaps you should walk a little. You can lean on me...." He was tall and bent ever so slightly as to catch a whiff of the hyacinth scented perfume she wore in her hair and of course to peer down at her chest. She was being shy, but she was also exaggerating her condition to receive more attention. "Is it better?" All better. A kiss on the forehead, then the lips and finally the invitation she had been waiting for soon followed: "See you tonight...."

The servants prepared the "blue room" which was destined to be for the emperor's amorous encounters. A bed was placed in the center of the room and was made to look like a monument, not too tall, but still placed on a small platform. On one of the neighboring walls, one could distinguish the outline of a doorway: it was the door that Napoleon III used to remain unseen as he walked in his night gown. The door opened and in the light, the shadow of the most powerful man in France could be distinguished. He took a step forward and closed the door behind him with a swift kick. He moved prudently in the darkness and managed to trip over a footstool, but he managed to find *Nicchia*'s embrace. She wrote in her diary: "He lowered himself.... I closed my eyes ... and destiny took its course...."[3]

---

[2] Marzia Ratti, *Tout ce qui s'appelle Castiglione c'est moi. La contessa di Castiglione e il suo tempo*, Turin 2000.
[3] *Ibidem.*

Once she was freed of all her frills and liberated from the grandeur of that figure, she added: "When he left, I heard, in the distance, the clock strike two … it had struck one-thirty when he had arrived…." Barely a half hour was needed to begin weaving the fabric of a Piedmont that needed to grow at all costs.

Historians are quick to dismiss any influence that the Countess of Castiglione may have had in matters regarding Italy's independence. Soon they will say she did not exist at all. This happens because truly professional historians want the papers, the seals and stamps that for sensitive reasons, in this case, cannot, obviously, be found.

They are also impossible to find because when the lady died, the French Secret Service searched her home in Paris and burned everything[4] they did not want to become public knowledge. At the same time, the Italian Secret Service did the same thing in her home in La Spezia. To be honest, her home in Italy had already been visited two other times by very bizarre thieves. They only seemed to steal books and notebooks and burned them on the site where they had found them.

Instead, it would be more plausible to believe that it was truly the Contessa of Castiglione who paved the way for the collaboration between the Savoy family and Napoleon III. It is well known that, as far as results are concerned, bed sheets are worth ten, one hundred, perhaps even one thousand "business lunches."

Does this all foil the plans of the "weavers," heroes, and martyrs of the *Risorgimento*? Without asking for anything in return, she took advantage of her skills as a seductress and gave it her best effort with her enthusiasm and patriotism, though she insisted upon choosing her battlefield herself.

During the Paris Peace Conference, Lord Henry Cowley, the British ambassador, informed Minister Clarendon of the French emperor's "interest" in the beautiful Virginia *Nicchia* of Castiglione. In his opinion, this liaison would have an enormous influence on

---

[4] Adriana Beverini e Pia Spangiari, *Virginia Oldoini contessa di Castiglione*, La Spezia 1999.

the conference's outcome. The Austrian envoy, Joseph Alexander Hubner, was even more worried and warned his government of Napoleon III's "dangerous passion."[5]

At that time, she often visited Turin's embassy in France and used encrypted messages to communicate with home. She also received her mail here. Urbano Rattanzi, who was not known for his refined ability with words especially regarding sentimental matters, dubbed her the "golden vulva of our *Risorgimento*."

The affair, which became quite fiery, began to waver on April 2nd, 1857 when the emperor was attacked by a hired assassin[6] on the landing of his lover's apartment. This attack was very likely orchestrated by the Empress Eugenia who began to tire of her husband's affair and thought it appropriate to bring it to an end. If this was her intention then she succeeded because the affair came to a steady halt and finally ceased altogether. *Nicchia* continued to frequent the world of high society though she used her charm more prudently.

Besides, Piedmont's objectives were being met thanks to her help.

On the evening of July 20th, 1858 Cavour arrived at Plombières to meet with Napoleon III. He left with a fake passport with the intention of concealing his identity though perhaps he should have taken other precautions. Too many people in Turin were aware of his mission and they knew about it because he had told them so. He added a few details here and there, according to whom he spoke.

This appointment was the result of intense diplomatic activity. To further ensure a positive outcome, the emperor's personal doctor, Henri Conneau, attended as well. In the emperor's entourage, he was a particularly important proponent of the "Piedmontese Party" and a specialist in foreign policy that dealt with areas south of the Alps. These matters pertained to his youth. Conneau was

---

[5] Henri De Ideville, *Il re, il conte e la Rosina. Diario pettegolo di un diplomatico alla corte dei Savoia* (edited by Guido Artom), Milan 1966.
[6] Raffaele Del Castello, *Napoleone III, l'ultimo sovrano romantic*, Milano 1933.

born in Milan and had lived for a long time in Florence. He refused to speak Italian with Cavour, who often responded in French because he happened to have a better command of that language. Even Napoleon III felt that a piece of his heart belonged across that border. He had been to Italy when he was exiled after the fall of the other Napoleon, Bonaparte. He had actually adhered to the principles of the Carbonarist movement and in Emilia Romagna, had actually participated in the first of the insurrections. He was familiar with the issues that were important to patriots from Turin, Milan, Rome, and Naples and he considered himself a good friend of Italy.

However, it would be wrong to think that the decision to overthrow the governments of the existing states depended exclusively upon the noble appeal of romantic sentimentalism.

Perhaps only a small part can attributed to this sentimentalism. The true reason behind Paris' intervention in Piedmont was the desire to redraw the borders of Europe, not only those of Italy. Napoleon III wanted to go to war with Austria so that the "Latin race could triumph over the Germanic one". He wanted to be at the head of the class again. He wanted back that leadership that had been taken from him over the course of the previous fifty years. Austria needed to be defeated[7] in order for this to take place and therefore Turin's ambitions could be granted. In the game of international politics, Cavour had his role.

In Plombières, amidst the woods that surrounded the city upon descending from Ballon d'Alsace, an agreement was reached between the two statesmen.

They agreed[8] to establish a Northern State with the Kingdom of Piedmont and would add the regions of Veneto and Lombardy as an appanage for the Savoys. The Center of Italy could have constituted the second block that could have been granted, if possible, to the emperor's cousin, Jerome Napoleon. The South could have remained in the hands of the Bourbon or could have been

---

[7] Eugenio De Rienzo, *Napoleone III*, Rome 2010.
[8] Arrigo Petacco, *Il regno del nord, il sogno di Cavour infranto da Garibaldi*, Milan 2009.

granted to some illustrious relative in the Parisian court, such as Luciano Murat. He was the son of Joachim Murat, who had been the king of Naples at the beginning of the century but who had been murdered during the insurrection.

The agreement was to be sealed by the marriage of the daughter of Victor Emanuel II, Clotilde, with Jerome Napoleon. Speaking in strictly humane terms, this would have been a difficult pill to swallow. Clotilde was barely sixteen years old and was a God-fearing little girl that was consumed by her daily prayers and devotion to the Virgin Mary. Jerome was a blaspheming womanizer who frequently visited nightclubs and frequented the dancers there. He slept through the day so that he could be ready to visit the most luxurious brothels at night. His nickname was *Plon-Plon*.

On a purely diplomatic level, the marriage was perfect. The Savoys would have been able to directly govern their Northern Kingdom and half of the Central Kingdom through blood relations. Cavour had also thought to arrange another wedding between Victor Emanuel II and a Russian princess. The favorable opinion gained from the czar would have served to further cement the alliance. The king did not want to hear of it. He would take anyone to bed but, officially, he only wanted that barrel-shaped Rosina. She was curvy like a traditional peasant was supposed to be and would dress herself up to resemble a lampshade almost as if to make up for her miserable upbringing.

There were a few more issues to be dealt with. How would France be compensated for its contribution? Cavour was obliged to give Napoleon III Nice and the region of Savoy, which are located on the other side of the Alps.

Also, how would they go about starting the war? For reasons of international plausibility, France could not assume the responsibility of declaring war. It was necessary that their intervention be a "defensive" one and therefore it was necessary to provoke the Austrians. In this manner, it would be the Austrians who would have attacked and placed themselves in the difficult diplomatic position of "aggressor."

Cavour had no rivals in this plot and already had elaborated a strategic plan. An area bordering Piedmont could be provoked to the point of insurrection. The rebels then would turn to Turin asking for help. Victor Emanuel II would respond negatively but would criticize the Viennese government to the point that the Austrians would have to attack.

Where could they light the fuse? They had initially thought of Tuscany, but this hypothesis was scrapped by Cavour. "The Etruscan race does not have enough energy," he mused.[9] Perhaps it would be better to consider Massa Carrara which was also near the Savoy border and where there was also a litigious cell that would be perfect to start a patriotic row.

They signed the agreement, which was to remain secret. Cavour was forced to lie to the entire government. He told the Parliament of the mutual understanding between Turin and Paris but remained silent about the specific terms that bound them. He specifically said nothing regarding the surrendering of the Savoy region, which he knew to be unacceptable to the population there. The soldiers from the region of Savoy were the best in the entire Savoy army. How could one ask them to fight for a State that, in case of victory, would deny them citizenship?

Cavour swore on his honor and that of his country that Piedmont's territorial integrity was not in question.[10] His declarations, however, no longer convinced anyone. The Parliament demanded that an "elected" commission be allowed to interrogate the Prime Minister privately, in order to obtain the necessary information in secrecy. Cavour, with no scruples whatsoever, continued to falsely swear that no territories would be ceded.

To ensure a positive outcome to the whole affair, it was necessary to appear trustworthy to the eyes of France and, at the same time, to irritate the Austrians to the point where they would be obliged to declare war.

---

[9] Denis Mack Smith, *Cavour, il grande tessitore dell'unià d'Italia*, cit.
[10] *Ibidem.*

This meant that they needed to appear half conservative and half revolutionary. The effort required to maintain this equilibrium was tremendous.

France asked for vigorous actions to be taken against the extremists of the time, the followers of Mazzini and those who resorted to the use of bombs, who exacerbated the political climate and disturbed the conservative government of Napoleon III.

Around the middle of June in 1857 the Parisian secret service informed Piedmont that Genoa was preparing an insurrection. What a revelation! This information managed to be the type of secret that became common knowledge almost instantly. Carlo Pisacane was the organizer of the expedition by Giuseppe Mazzini's suggestion and with funding gathered from those patriots who had been exiled.

Cavour must have been informed about the plot, but was undecided on how to go about it. He had hoped that the organizer planned to act quickly. On June 25th, a maniple of revolutionaries boarded the steamship *Cagliari*, which belonged to the Ligurian company known as the *Rubattino*, and seized it, thereby setting off the insurrection that history remembers as the "Sapri Expedition". It wound up being a massacre. "Three hundred strong youths died." When it was all over, Camillo Benso did his best to lay the blame upon everyone else including the police, which was deemed to be "inefficient." This was all deliberately set up to please France, who had requested such repressive measures. Cavour defined Mazzini as the "true leader of a gang of assassins" and that he "collaborated with Austria". He complained that London had welcomed him and had offered him hospitality for too long. So that his words would have more impact, he arranged for a large group of extremists to be rounded up[11] and, after reaching an agreement with the United States, had them shipped off to the new world. In this manner, he was able to place an ocean between the extremists and his own plans.

---

[11] *Ibidem.*

Felice Orsini's assassination attempt on Napoleon III proved to be more difficult to handle. On January 13, 1858 he launched two bombs at the carriage that carried Napoleon III. This was shocking to Cavour. Orsini had previously been in contact with the Piedmontese government, which had financed his projects with the usual funds from the secret service.[12] Turin filled another ship with rabble-rousers, even if they were only presumed to be so, and shipped them off to America.

The French felt obliged to request more definitive measures.

In the meantime, it became necessary to change the orientation of the government. Cavour had administrated the State's politics along with the assistance of Urbano Rattazzi. This political orientation could be considered Center-Left or even Left-Center. This was too Left for Paris. Cavour implored that this re-orientation of the government not be made known to the public so as to avoid being accused of being at the service of another country. He immediately complied with the wishes of Napoleon III, however, and proceeded to fire Rattazzi from his post as Minister of Internal Affairs, despite the fact that he had always been a loyal collaborator and a precious friend. Then again, when has politics ever shown itself to be grateful to anyone? Several ministers, Castelli, Farini and Lanza, did not approve the cold-blooded firing of Rattazzi and believed that such an act reeked of unjustifiable subterfuges.

France was still not satisfied and requested more important measures taken in the press regarding the freedom of expression. Cavour's words made him appear to be a liberal but he became a man of the government and he accepted the idea to censor immoral books and any other book that was politically suspicious. He intercepted private letters and justified the existence of a secret police. He adopted the practice of bribing journalists with money that came from undisclosed accounts.

When the French requested other stringent measures, Cavour replied that he needed more time, but to show his good will, in

---

[12] Alfredo Venturi, *L'uomo delle bombe. La vita e I tempi di Felice Orsini terrorista e gentiluomo*, Milan 2009.

the hopes that he would meet with their approval, he called for the investigation of a newspaper in Genoa. *L'Italia del Popolo* was a newspaper that was inspired by Mazzini's ideas. It printed four hundred copies, half of which were distributed for free. It was a completely harmless publication but needed to be silenced to prove a point. The orders given were final, "It will not be necessary to worry too much about the legal means employed to attain the objective." National interest required severe measures. Four of the directors were jailed (and then released because there was no evidence against them). Fifty issues were seized in a few months. When the administration finally waved a white flag upon the matter, all of the other newspapers demonstrated their solidarity against this abuse.

A gag-law was necessary.[13] The Chamber of Deputies issued him a warning. He appeared to be too openly obedient to foreign powers. Cavour then took it upon himself to speak to each single deputy in order to convince them to support the common interest by voting in favor of his new law.

After all, Piedmont forced itself to please everyone.

It had allowed the Russians to build a naval base near Nice, which gained them disapproval from London. The Crimean War had been declared necessary to keep the czar's fleets out of the Mediterranean. Cavour had requested permission to loan a navy frigate to tame the Taiping rebels in China. In India, he offered England that same frigate against the revolutionaries declaring our "profound sympathy towards the suffering and heroic behavior demonstrated by the English patriots in India."

The freedom and nationalism that were defended in Europe were not valid in Asia.

In the end, the alliance with France took a turn for the worst.

---

[13] Denis Mack Smith, *Cavour, il grande tessitore dell'unità d'Italia*, cit.

CHAPTER 6

Finally, Camillo Cavour Heard the Rumble of the Cannons

"La Marmora! Prepare your cannons![1] Because we are going to Milan ... and perhaps Venice...." Count Camillo Benso of Cavour was excited. He was satisfied of the trust he had obtained from France and was certain that he could play his cards to best suit his interests.

Just to make sure he absolutely infuriated Austria, he decided to fortify Alexandria. This expense had been authorized with a decree a few days after the start of the Parliament's vacation. What was the purpose of this? To postpone any form of debate about this fortification until after the groundwork had been laid. The deputies did not need to approve, but merely ratify. The criticisms that followed this act were quite violent in regards to the method implemented even before the matter to be discussed was even addressed. The majority of them were willing to accept anything so why try to deceive them all with subterfuges that bordered illegality[2]?

They were going towards a war with reckless reluctance. Napoleon knew that the French public disapproved. Why should they offer their men and weapons to a tiny State that was trapped by the Alps? The "Anti-Italian Party," spearheaded by the Empress Eugenia[3] was spreading doubt and evil ideas so as to ward off the risk of a conflict that would inevitably cost France precious lives and funds.

Even in Piedmont there seemed to be no intention to set their troops in motion. General Adolphe Niel, in Turin, verified this

---

[1] Alfonso La Marmora, *Un episodio del Risorgimento italiano*, Florence 1875.
[2] Denis Mack Smith, *Cavour, il grande tessitore dell'unita` d'Italia*, cit.
[3] Paul Gueriot, *Napoleone III*, Paris 1933.

personally when he went to authorize the military action. "With the exception of Cavour, Rattazzi and a half-dozen other mad-men[4], the rest of Piedmont is against the war." Even General La Marmora, the Minister of War, was tepid in regards to the matter: he should have been the first to arm his artillery to drive out the Austrians from Lombardy and the Veneto regions.

When the dissent was particularly vigorous, Cavour resolved the problem by ignoring it. The Count continued down his path trying to fuel the escalation that was intended to spark the war.

In the meantime, it became necessary to prove that political change was required and firmly desired: the "cells" that were Pro-Piedmont from Milan to Florence to Modena and Bologna, were granted the freedom to organize protests against the governments in power and, contemporaneously, declare their support for the Savoy monarchs. It was necessary to make themselves heard but with moderation, without compromising themselves. They were to ask for reforms but without exaggerating.

Cavour wanted a not-so-revolutionary revolution. The actors in these constructed revolts complained because the orders they received from Turin were unclear. The patriots practically stood still. Luigi Carlo Farini, who was the head of the "National Society" that was supposed to carry the flag of ideology for the Unification of Italy, was placed in charge of 94 committees that were scattered throughout Italy. In reality, this was all a bunch of smoke: in Modena, everyone "is asleep," in Reggio, "they are not awake."[5] No one does anything in Tuscany, "when four or five influential people could get all of the work done." In Bologna, "the committee does not even meet, the newspaper is not distributed, and nothing is done because no one wants to do anything."[6] It seemed

---

[4] Denis Mack Smith, *Cavour, il grande tessitore dell'unità d'Italia*, cit.
[5] Giuseppe La Farina, *Scritti politici (raccolti e pubblicati da Ausonio Franchi)*, Milan 1870. Letter written on December 5, 1859 addressed to Gaetano Braglia in Scandiano.
[6] *Ibidem.* Letter written on November 23, 1859 addressed to the friar Filippo Bartolomeo in Messina.

as if to attain the Italy that everyone wanted "only the gods had to fight." Mankind had other things to think about.

Cavour imagined provoking the Austrians by harboring refugees that came from other regions that volunteered to fight in the war for independence that seemed imminent. Amongst the Neapolitans were Carlo Poerio and Luigi Settembrini. They had just been released from the Bourbon prison and seemed to be a little too fat to have undergone all of the torture and suffering that was reported on their behalf.

Petruccelli della Gattina expressed his perplexity.[7] "When we riled Europe against the Bourbon, we needed to personify the evils of that horrible dynasty. We needed a living, breathing victim. We invented Poerio. The real Poerio took the invented Poerio seriously. We constructed his image in twelve years through the use of articles that we wrote for fifteen cents per line. Those who read about him took him seriously. Even the media that became our accomplice took him seriously and believed every word we said. Holy capers! Even Cavour took him seriously....!"

They believed that twenty thousand soldiers would arrive, lowered their expectations to ten thousand, and finally resigned themselves to receiving three thousand. It was a meager amount and it was difficult to avoid any ironic comments. "Twenty million human beings that truly feel oppressed," Lord Cowley from England underlined, "would certainly provide more than a few thousand recruits for the army that aims to protect them all." What a disappointment. It was even more so because the Piedmontese had been attracted by the higher salaries offered by Austria and so they crossed the borders and aided them in building their own fortifications.

Negative signs arrived from abroad. Victor Emanuel II's speech, famous for his utterance that "we are not indifferent to shouts of agony," was negatively viewed in England. The English Minister of Foreign Affairs, James Howard Malmesbury, activated the chan-

---

[7] Massimo Viglione, *op.cit.*

cellery in order to avoid a conflict that his government believed to be inconvenient and dangerous.

There was a real risk that "peace would break out." The European diplomacy retained the right to intervene and proposed a conference so that the issue of Piedmont could be discussed and excluded Piedmont from the discussions.

Cavour attempted to react but only managed to talk nonsense. He threatened to ally himself with real revolutionaries. No one took him seriously. He sent secret agents to Belgrade and Bucharest to organize an illegal weapons trade which was to spark an insurrection in Hungary. He promised to deliver 100,000 rifles. He managed to deliver 20,000 when the entire matter was over. That tiny arsenal managed to be used for an entirely different purpose.

In the end, he was forced to give up and accept the European diktat. Piedmont was asked to disarm itself and this would have spelled its end. Pier Carlo Boggio, an unrivaled controversialist, wrote in a significantly entitled booklet in 1959, *Fra un mese*.... "The State increased its public debt by five hundred million [...] falsified its budget [...] changed its actions from their original focus [...] imposed upon itself a path that was different from its natural orbit [...] placed its institutions at risk [...] sacrificed numerous lives of its children in the name of the glorious objective that it proposed for itself: the liberation of Italy. In these past years, there has been no sacrifice of blood or money that appeared too excessive."[8]

This bluff, which was played out on the chessboards of the chancelleries of the world, had been discovered and called out.

A page from the diary of Giuseppe Massari gives a clear image of the tension present at that time. "The meetings of the Council of Ministers of yesterday and today have been stormy. All of the count's colleagues reproached him for having trusted too much. Cavour stated that since Napoleon wanted peace, "*je le subis Napo-*

---

[8] Denis Mack Smith, *Cavour, Il grande tessitore dell'unità d'Italia*, cit.

lèon." (I subjected myself to Napoleon) He also stated that if English politics triumphed in this instance that all would be lost."[9]

The great "weaver" of the fabric of our country found himself alone. It is possible that he even contemplated suicide.

He spent one day and two nights fidgeting and burning papers. He paced his office with long strides and spoke to himself. He threw up his arms and insulted invisible enemies and tried to cajole imperceptible allies. In the end, the secretary Michelangelo Castelli found the courage to face him: "Must I think that Count Cavour desires to desert the battlefield and abandon everyone?"[10] This question, which was offered with no lexical intermediation, must have had the effect of a whip because the answer it provoked appeared to be quite reassuring, "We will face everything, and we will always do so together."

Right when the political climate seemed to be favoring Vienna, Austria unexpectedly managed to injure itself. It decided to attack Piedmont with the false conviction that it would be able to free itself of its burden.

Piedmont was given three days to respond to the ultimatum given and Cavour used that time down to the last second while all of the alliances in Europe turned upside down. With this aggressive attack, the Austro-Hungarian Empire could instantly be accused of wrongdoing and Piedmont gained the sympathy of many governments, including France and England. Even the Parisian "Anti-Italian Party" had to surrender in light of the change of events.

In that time period, a *liaison* occurred between the Piedmontese envoy in Paris, Costantino Nigra, and the Empress Eugenia. This revelation came from a historical novel called *Ottocento* and cites an encounter between the two on April 22, 1859 in a home in Rue de Saint-Roch. Nigra had brought his young son, Lionello, with him. When his son was an adult, he recounted the afternoon he was introduced to the empress of France. He was too small to understand at the time why his father chose to bring him to the

---

[9] Giuseppe Massari, *Letter Politiche*, Trani 1895.
[10] Michelangelo Castelli, *Ricordi* (edited by Luigi Chiala), Turin 1888.

meeting. Perhaps he did not want to be alone with the empress for fear of what she could have asked him about the extraordinary event that was happening in those very hours. It was a victory for him and a defeat for her. The boy recounted that his father consoled her. The lady had hugged the child tenderly and proceeded to extend her hand to Nigra, who bowed before her. The young boy remembered that they "proceeded to walk to their hotel on that calm evening. My father held me by my hand and talked and talked ... his tone was as happy as usual but his face had a hint of sadness in it."[11]

It goes without saying that there were many risks for Piedmont. Turin had no defense and the people of the city were in a state of panic. They feared that their enemies were capable of crossing the border, defeating the Savoy troops, and invading the State.

Cavour had taken the precaution of moving the government to Genoa. In those days, the nobles left the capital. The most worried people of all were the generals and high-ranking officials who gave their respective families the order to move to their country homes, as far away as possible. The danger was averted by the Austrians themselves, when they proceeded to declare a war which they did not fight.

The Austrian Ambassador Hubner, who was in Paris, wrote to Count Buol, his Prime Minister, to complain about the army's laziness: "Pain, impatience, and rage for the hesitation of General Gyulai. Good Heavens! All he must do is cross the Ticino River, attack the Piedmontese and destroy them ... yet he continues to stand still, with his weapon at his feet, because it is raining!"

The commander of the Viennese army was taking his time because he was convinced that Prussia would also enter the war and that the outcome of the conflict would be determined on the banks of the Rhine River. The army's supply wagons moved slowly and wound up getting mired in the rice fields near the areas of Lomellina and Novara.

---

[11] Annabella Cabiati, *Op. cit.*

The French emperor had promised 120,000 soldiers and he arrived with just that amount, crossing from Marseille to Genoa by sea and climbing towards Milan. Napoleon III brought his troops to fight against Austria. It was a terrible clash during which he and his men bore the brunt of the battle resulting in the deaths of thousands.

Piedmont and the Savoy troops made cameo appearances. Victor Emanuel II, Cavour, and the high ranking commanders of the State, had assured that they would have brought 150,000 men to the battlefield but they were scarcely able to put together an army of 50,000. Half of those who were enlisted, called to arms by some fabricated means, did not even answer to the draft and avoided ever wearing a uniform.

Matters were even worse regarding rifles and ammunition.[12] Those who were unarmed were placed behind the front lines and were forced to gather their weapons from any fallen fellow soldier.

The first days of battle were pure torture for the soldiers. They needed to reach the front lines by wading across the Adda and Oglio Rivers. The heavy rains had made the waters rise and the pontoniers did not have enough material to construct a bridge with boats. So they were forced to go "up and down the rivers searching for a possible passage and even though many of them began moving before dawn, there were still troops that arrived after midnight." Even the following stop, Castagneto, despite being only twenty kilometers away, resulted in the loss of 700 men. They were exhausted from carrying their cumbersome backpacks and from wearing clothing that was too heavy.

The soldiers limped because the leather on the spats they wore to cross the rivers, upon drying, became hard as wood and cut the tops of their feet. This is why the French used canvas instead of leather. General Paolo Solaroli recounted this to Victor Emanuel II, who replied, "La Marmora knows everything ... why did he not know this....?"

---

[12] Piero Pieri, *Storia militare del Risorgimento*, Turin 1962.

The Sardinian army did not have any plans for a war that it was allegedly preparing to have for the past ten years. In 1848-1849, there were no topographical maps and the same remained true in 1859. The officials believed that they could solve the problem by following the rare road signs along the way and by extorting information from any farmers they might meet along the way.

The army did not have a sufficient number of ambulances and the pontoniers were also lacking equipment (which was absolutely necessary when crossing a region like Lombardy which has many rivers). The field artillery was insufficient and when the time came to attack Peschiera, they realized that their best weapons had been left behind in their depots. The cavalry led by General Callisto Balbo Bertone of Sambuy could not move: their horses had lost their shoes and would have risked injury after only a few kilometers.

The officials were belligerent in times of peace and inept in times of war, such as this one, and in any other war. They proved their inadequacy, starting from the top.

"The greatest risk that we are taking," wrote Cavour to Nigra, "is not in fighting the Austrians, but leaving the King at the head of the army when he cannot command more than one regiment."[13]

Madame Rattazzi wrote: "Enrico Morrozzo della Rocca was Chief of the Army General Staff, which was a title that should have gone to General La Marmora. Even though La Marmora was not a top notch general he was a fire bolt compared to the phlegmatic Della Rocca."[14] Della Rocca had just so happened to find himself in this lofty position because he had two advantages in his favor: he was a perfect member of the royal court and he was the husband of Countess Irene, the lover of Victor Emanuel.

The army stopped for three days in Brescia and then proceeded on its way towards Lonato.

---

[13] Camillo Benso Conte di Cavour, *Nuove letter inedite* (edited by Eduard Mayor), Turin 1895.

[14] Maria Laetitia Rattazzi, *Rattazzi et son temps: documents inedits, correspondenance, souvenirs intimes*, Paris 1881.

The king decided to spend his time fishing in Desenzano in the company of two assistants and two members of the Army General Staff. He liked the town and that was deemed a good enough reason to justify the establishment of his headquarters there. No one objected that it was an enchanting place to spend a vacation but it was entirely too far away from the battlefields and therefore unsuitable.

The king dispatched communications.

He wrote to Cavour to complain about Napoleon III: "We have been subjected to new tribulations: the worthy ruler changes his mind and then changes it again and wants things which are impossible."[15] He wrote to Eugenio Carignano to complain about Cavour: "This time the Count has lost his mind!" He also wrote to Rattazzi to complain about everyone: "The titles have all been assigned unjustly: they all should be removed from the army either for theft or other crimes ... begin to do this and report to me...."

Cavour was counting on 50,000 Italian soldiers that served in the Austrian army. In actuality, the number was much lower and in Solferino, the 16th Infantry Regiment, which was almost exclusively composed by Venetians, "fought with tenacity" against the French. They deserved a mention in the annals.

In a page of a diary that was never intended for publication, Massari, who disclosed a private comment made by Ambassador Hudson, noted that "the Lombard population showed absolute apathy and in some cases outright hostility towards the Sardinian-Piedmontese army."[16]

General Paolo Salaroli from Novara narrated that he arrived with his men in Palazzolo, after a march that had lasted 17 hours with no food. "The locals did not even offer us a glass of water. What wonderful compatriots we have come to free!"

The stories that can be told come from all sides and speak indifferently about patriots and conservatives, Pro-Piedmont advocates and partisans fighting for Austria. Carlo Cattaneo recalled:

---

[15] Adriano Viarengo, *op. cit.*
[16] Giuseppe Massari, *Diario dalle cento voci*, Bologna 1959.

"In 1859, Milan remained immobile in the wake of the battle, when an atom could have tipped the balance to one side or the other. In 1848, Como attacked and killed two thousand Austrians and in 1859, it welcomed the victorious Garibaldi with its doors closed, in a tomb-like silence."[17]

The "Times" wrote that the "unrest in Lombardy was a Piedmontese invention." The war correspondent, who followed the troops, added that not only was patriotism non-existent in Lombardy but also in Piedmont. After he rode for 140 miles and after having spoken to farmers, he wrote that "the reports on the animosity of the Italians towards the Austrians were completely false." The people complained about Cavour's government, which "burdened them with taxes in order to maintain an army that was well above its means."

On June 4, 1859, the first battle took place in Magenta. Nicola Nisco, who was commissioned to write six volumes so as to (properly) tell Italy's history, most likely by the king, was able to attribute the merit of that day to Victor Emanuel II, the intrepid commander. In actuality, the Piedmontese commander was 12 kilometers away and his troops did not participate all that much: they reported no injuries.

The painting that depicts the king brandishing his unsheathed sword as he leads his cavalry over San Martino's crest is the result of a court painter's adulation.

The king spent the entire day of the battle wandering from Castel Venzago to Mount Castellero and then to Lonato. He was sought by messengers so that they could inform him that the fighting had begun and they found him at Castel Castellero, tremendously fatigued by the great heat. He was sweating due to the great effort it took to move his entourage to and fro, and was lying underneath a tree with his jacket open and a cigar in his mouth[18] seeking some reprieve. When he finally joined the victorious

---

[17] Carlo Cattaneo, *Epistolario* (edited by Rinaldo Caddeo), Florence 1949-1956.
[18] Paolo Solaroli di Briona, *Diario*, Turin 1888 (this was published anonymously and inserted in the "Memoirs" of Michelangelo Castelli).

troops, the battle was over. Not for nothing, Napoleon III considered him qualified enough to be called a sergeant and the Frenchman d'Ideville confirmed that effectively, he was not worth much more.

The regiments of Vicenza and Verona, who had sided with the Viennese army, retreated. Speaking of irredentism and feelings of "belonging" when these soldiers had been invited to desert their armies to join the ranks of Piedmont, which was expanding to include the rest of Italy, they replied that they were loyal subjects of Austria.[19]

Victory came because the French won. The decisive battle occurred in Solferino.

The Austrian emperor, Franz Josef, was not able to take command because he, along with the Army General Staff, took the wrong path. Without clarity, the commanders of the two Austrian armies behaved autonomously and therefore operated with no hope of ever coordinating their actions. The clash was a bloody one. The French soldiers, when the time came to use their bayonets, removed their backpacks to have more liberty of movement. When they returned to retrieve them, the backpacks were nowhere to be found. They had been stolen.

In his war report, the Swiss reporter Jean-Henri Dunant noted that "The Lombards are hungry for shoes which they brutally tear from the swollen feet of the cadavers."

The Piedmontese army fought at San Martino.

Twenty thousand Austrians headed by General Benedek held off the attacks of fifty thousand Piedmontese, who were amateurs when it came to launching an attack.

It would have been necessary to strike first with the artillery and then to move the infantry, but the artillery was far away and a "Garibaldi" style attack was employed which called for repeated bayonet charges.

---

[19] *Ibidem.*

Victor Emanuel, to demonstrate that he was fearless and to incite the soldiers to fight (which was actually the duty of a higher ranking official) rode his horse for the entire day. He moved to various "hot-spots" during the battle. At 3:30PM the French had won while the Piedmontese had not actually made a move yet.

These were isolated attacks. General Govone stated: "Our troops were employed as soon as they reached their destination, so it was impossible to organize a coordinated attack." Fifty years later, the official headquarters of the army issued its sentence: "The troops were admirable and devoted, but they were penalized by a lack of coordinated action."

San Martino was taken with a five-hour delay when Benedek received the order to retreat, which he reluctantly did. What was not obtained on the battlefield was obtained in the rhetorical narration of the events.

Napoleon was convinced that it would be opportune to abandon the effort at this point. In France, the public opinion was boiling over and Prussia was becoming agitated along the edge of the Rhine. It was better to stop after the initial damage was done.

Napoleon III and Franz Josef agreed to a *demi-paix* (a "half-peace") that turned into an all-round peace on July 11th after a discussion that lasted around an hour in the Gandini-Morelli-Bugna Villa in Villafranca.

The French emperor sent Victor Emanuel II a "private and personal" message to encourage him to move in accordance with the agreements that had been reached. He summarized, "Italy should be formed by many independent states that are united by federalism. Each of these states must adopt its own system of representation and make reforms as necessary. The resulting Confederation will ratify the notion of an Italian nation that will have one flag, one system of customs taxes, and one currency.[20] Its administrative center will be Rome and it will be composed of representatives that are nominated by the monarchs. Their names will be given to the Chambers so that, in this sort of Diet, the influence of

---

[20] Massimo Viglione, *op. cit.*

those families suspected of favoring Austria will be balanced by the result of the ensuing election. The honorary presidency would be offered to the Holy Father, and in this manner Europe's religious inclinations will be satisfied."

At the end, he offered his political opinion: "I believe that unity will follow unification, not the other way around."

Cavour viewed this request to halt as a betrayal. He kicked all of the chairs in his way and with cheeks that were even rosier than usual, proceeded to make a series of lewd comments worthy of any sailor. He resigned from his post, which was offered to La Marmora even though the more important minister was Rattazzi. He was destined to leave his mark on this brief and unlucky cabinet.

In their agreement, Paris and Vienna established that Lombardy would be handed over to Piedmont and reaffirmed that Italy was to become a confederation. Austria, who would control the Veneto region, would be an integral part of the project. Yet it was the presence of Austria that wound up being the weakest link in this structure. How does one go about living as "equals" with the enemy, by definition?

CHAPTER 7

The North Was Betrayed: the Master-State is Born

"This was not how the agreement was made ... you had assumed different duties...." Gabrio Casati, who was nominated Minister of Education in order to give the government an
image that better represented its newly formed State, slapped his
resignation letter on the table after pronouncing these words.[1] He
complained that there was too much of a hurry to transfer Piedmontese statutes and institutions to Lombardy. The initial idea
was to fuse the two regions together by taking the best of what
each had to offer so that a synthesis could be reached that was not
only agreeable to both, but perhaps even virtuous.

There were plenty of studies and projects prepared on the subject. A special commission had been created and presided over by
Count Cesare Giulini della Porta from Milan. He was a reputable
patriot, having been a part of the provisionary government following the Five Day Insurrection in 1848. The definitive document
was drawn up exclusively by Lombard citizens who had exam-
ined all of the issues at hand without any prejudice. It was for this
reason that the conclusions of this document were deemed to be
"interesting." They had painted an accurate picture of the socio-
political scene of the new State and they proceeded to illustrate in
detail what needed to be done to blend the new provinces together. They took the existing administrations into consideration because in certain instances they functioned very well.

Local governments were to be respected and encouraged to
improve themselves. They were considered protagonists of a virtuous cycle and this seemed to be the right recipe to obtain significant practical results. Even the intellectual elite of Turin were in

---

[1] Denis Mack Smith, *Cavour, il grande tessitore dell'unità d'Italia*, cit.

agreement that this was the right path to follow. A study that had been conducted the previous year, in 1858, by Teodoro di Santa Rosa, viewed the expansion of Piedmont in the same fashion and proposed identical solutions.

The government (but perhaps it would be better to specify only Rattazzi) stated that it approved the notions written in those documents and declared that it would act accordingly. In reality, it behaved as though it had never taken those notions into consideration. Quite the contrary, the government took on the behavior of a master who decides, arranges, and issues orders, expecting them to be carried out.

The first blow delivered to the construction of a federalized State, with adequate institutions, came from the guilty conscience of whoever announced that changes would be made without ever truly having the intention of making them.

Rattazzi decided to extend the civil, penal, and procedural code to Lombardy. He ensured the approval of decrees that allowed for (and in some cases obligated) the interference of the State in provincial and town administrations. He promulgated regulations[2] regarding education that had contents that were more centralized in concept than the previous Boncompagni law, which had provisions that were destined to remain effective well into the new century and would be retouched during the Fascist Regime by the Gentile Reforms.

The Lombards felt betrayed. They were not being treated as equals and were not even considered capable of executing the most trivial administrative practices. For each government position that became available, a Piedmontese arrived to fill it. Occasionally the choice revealed itself as inadequate and the "new" director wound up being a nuisance.

It was impossible not to complain about an administration like the Austrian one, which was efficient by definition, which had been substituted by the Savoy one that managed to inch forward.

---

[2] Cesare Cantù, *Della indipendenza italiana*, Turin 1872-1877.

It appeared to be idling and did not give the impression that it could meet the people's needs.

Telegrams took ten days to reach their destinations and in February of 1861, the salaries of the previous month had not been paid. This revolution was provoked to substitute Vienna with Turin? The Hapsburgs had been kicked out to make way for the Savoy government?

The newspaper *La Perseveranza* reported, "Each of our observations is met with a reproach: you are municipalists, you are Lombards, you are youths that are frightened by the spectre of Piedmontism. We complain about the disorder in public institutions; the loss of other institutions, which had been rendered productive by experience; the precipitous application of laws that are not determined by need. What do they respond? You are Lombards, municipalists, small-town politicians."[3] It was impossible, according to the publication, to object that government positions were filled only upon Piedmontese recommendation and not by a contest open to the public. It was forbidden to highlight the error that was committed in transferring the headquarters of the Lombard railways to Turin. It was pointless, and in certain cases dangerous, to sustain the notion that the qualification of a French teacher could only be determined in the capital.

Il Pungolo, an evening newspaper that expressed itself using very frank terms, wanted to emphasize the incongruencies of the new justice reforms. "Turin has placed their hand on the system and disconnected it. It has altered the overarching economy and, may we add, in a very rash manner!"[4]

In the commotion of those months, it had not been possible (or perhaps there was no desire) to seek the approval of the Parliament. Everything needed to be done in a hurry. The new kingdom was born old with outdated laws that were implemented by a higher order. It was a Master-State.

---

[3] *La Perseveranza*, February 22, 1861.
[4] *Il Pungolo*, March 11, 1861.

The Lombards, who were well educated, wound up marginalizing themselves and became the spokespersons of the country's criticisms. This attitude irritated Piedmont. Those in Turin complained that each time they were forced to deal with a portion of the public that complained about their actions.

In 1859, the Milanese appeared to be afflicted with a superiority complex along with a guilt complex. The superiority came from their vigor and their proverbial abilities in the industrial and commercial spheres. The guilt dates back to the era of the Five Day Insurrection when, after the impetuosity of revolution wore off, it had seemed as though the Piedmontese were the enemy and not the Austrians. In 1849, Magenta refused to offer hospitality to General Ramorino's defeated troops. If one were to read the headlines of the newspapers at that time, it appeared as though the enemy was Charles Albert with his Savoy troops and not Radetzky and his. The wariness and mistrust from that time could only increase.

It is difficult to straighten a structure whose foundation is crooked. It is more likely that, should the construction continue, the architectural faults would worsen. In fact....

Lands that expressed no desire to be annexed were added to the "Unification."

First came the annexation of Tuscany, followed by that of the Emilia Romagna with the duchies of Modena and Parma. One really had to search to find any patriotic sentiment at all.

Could anyone testify to this? "I did not find any enthusiasm for the Unification of Italy anywhere, even though I had expected to find it because I had been deceived by the Piedmontese. Piedmont was viewed as a foreigner and conqueror."[5]

Another example: "The city of Massa has many citizens that support the Duchy ... many reside in the surrounding areas. Perhaps one can say that the Piedmontese domination is tolerated out

---

[5] Filippo Curletti, *La verità sugli uomini e sulle cose del regno d'Italia* (edited by Elena Bianchini Braglia), Modena 2009.

of fear. However, we would be inclined to take up our arms against ourselves....."[6]

Even the most patriotic Pro-Savoy supporters had to admit: "A single rifle shot would have sufficed to put an end to all of the conspiracies."[7]

The insurrections were not spontaneous. The Dukes and Grand Dukes abandoned their palaces. In their place arrived Luigi Carlo Farini in Modena, Adeodato Pallieri in Parma, Massimo d'Azeglio in Bologna, and Carlo Boncompagni in Florence.

Each of them arrived with their entourages of questionable reputation. They all behaved like Barbarians. They had no scruples: they destroyed, stole, killed, and tortured. But worst of all, they defiled the truth.

In Parma, Glauco Lombardi spent his entire life trying to recover at least a part of the furnishings that adorned Villa Farnese in Colorno, the Versailles of Italy. It had been brutally sacked by the Savoy victors.

It was not possible to recover anything from Modena. By order of Genevieffa Cassiani, the wife of the dictator Luigi Carlo Farini, the silverware was turned into ingots. A very minimal part of that small treasure made its way to Turin. The majority was kept by the new inhabitants that claimed it as compensation for their patriotism. In the papers it was reported that the Duke had escaped with everything, including his wardrobe and shoes, "leaving even the wine cellars empty."[8]

Farini, "a man from Emilia Romagna who had been ruined by poor investments," had the opportunity to rest his rear end on a real throne. It was said that he was the new Duke of Modena. He was reproached for the "reprehensible luxury" to which he had adapted his life. Massimo D'Azeglio was thankful that he did not

---

[6] *Ibidem.*
[7] *Ibidem.*
[8] Elena Bianchini Braglia (with Francesco Mario Agnoli, Franco Bampi, Ettore Beggiato, Lorenzo Del Boca, Gilberto Oneto), *L'unità divisa: 1861-2011. Parla l'Italia reale*, Rimini 2010.

need to deal with him: "I hope to never have to be subjected to his orders."

Everywhere, large, even enormous, sums of money disappeared with the same ease and speed with which they were taken from the coffers of the legitimate sovereigns.

Even at that time it was evident that "should a vote be called, with no cheats or external pressures or liberal terrorism, we are certain that the vast majority of the population would vote to detach themselves from Piedmont." It was for this obvious reason that it was necessary to prevent spontaneous elections.

The vote could not help but become, as was hoped, a plebiscite.

In Tuscany, a pressing media campaign was launched that declared "anyone who expressed anything but approval for the annexation would be declared an enemy of the State and would be punishable by death." The typographers were all busy printing the ballots promoting the annexation "and they had been warned that if any of them dared to publish any ballots in favor of separation there would be consequences."

The ballots were sent to farmers, who had no idea what to do with them. "We were told that that paper needed to be brought to the city in a certain place and whoever did not bring this paper would be fined. The farmers raced to bring the paper where it needed to go so that they would not have to pay a fine, without ever actually knowing what the paper was."

The vast majority of the population remained unaware of the call to vote.

The numbers showed that crowds of people showed up to vote and that the polls were mobbed. Everyone ran to express their desire to subject themselves to Savoy rule.

Actually, the time period that comprised the election passed by with little enthusiasm and with much indifference. Few actually went to cast their votes but those few were capable of expressing their preference even for those who had given up their right. Once the polls had closed, the workers began to count the votes and fill in any blank ballots "in favor of Piedmont, naturally." "I was physically present," assured Filippo Curletti, "and I speak because I experienced it all firsthand."[9]

The fact that the people did not know and did not understand what was happening "proved to be useful for fraudulent purposes and all control disappeared." All that needed to be done was to stuff the ballot box with votes that people never intended to express. In certain colleges "this massive introduction of absentee ballots was done with such little attention to detail that numbers revealed that there were more votes cast than registered voters. It became necessary to adjust everything when the official reports were released at the end of the vote count."

Even those who deceived without shame in order to obtain a vote of consensus from the people did not really want the Unification as it eventually became. Modena, Parma, and Emilia Romagna were lands that were very different from each other. Up until the previous day, they had been protected by borders and customs taxes that assured their sovereignty. How could they all be tied up in the same straitjacket?

Certainly, Bettino Ricasoli did not want to bring Tuscany into Piedmont. He expected to administrate autonomously to the point where he clashed with the central government of the time. "I don't like him...!" Massari recorded the scene of an angry Cavour who beat his head with his hands, shouting to release his aggravation. "He is wasting millions ... enormous sums ... he is so pedantic ... should he leave, we will all sing the *Te deum*...."[10] But he did not leave. The offered him the Presidency of the Senate, a very prestigious position that had no possibility of direct intervention in politics. As a result, they were met with a refusal.

Ricasoli was an interesting person. He was a moderately liberal baron in 1848, contrary to the changes in the democracy in 1849 to the point that his name was "often confused" with that of those who were intent upon restoring power to the Lorena dynasty.

---

[9] Filippo Curletti, *op.cit.*
[10] Giuseppe Massari, *Lettere politiche*, cit.

He is credited with defining the blend of grapes of Chianti wine, which is obtained by mixing the *malvasia* variety of grapes with the *sangiovese* variety. He was also responsible for the deaths of three out of his four children, two girls and one boy. He expected them to live in Spartan conditions, eating potatoes and "resisting the cold without covering themselves with heavy clothing and without covers in bed." Pneumonia took hold of them when they were still going to school.

He was tall and thin, irritable and vain. He always dressed in black and was frigid in all of his relations. It was practically impossible to reason with him. With their Tuscan sarcasm, the locals changed his name from *Bettino* to *Bet Bey*, so as to sound like the pasha of Tunisia whose methods and attitude he had adopted. It was also because of his character that Ricasoli did not want to rely on Turin the point that he expected to retain the right to make laws as far as his homeland was concerned.

"The other day," complained Cavour, "he sent us a decree in which he ordered the payment of six million to the towns of Tuscany for the Austrian occupation and the issuance of vouchers from the treasury for that amount." He was received by the king without informing the government of Turin first. He behaved as though he were a governor and expected that the prerogatives of administrative decentralization be ratified in such a way as to render them institutional.

However, after a few weeks of chatter, the Piedmont Law was ratified. The La Marmora-Rattazzi cabinet did not accept any suggestions and allowed no exceptions. Those who had hoped in federalism that respected tradition were disappointed and found themselves with an exasperated centralized government.

The government made it just in time to extend the application of the new laws to the provinces but was unable to face the Parliament and was forced to resign. It was deemed incapable of managing a transitional phase of that caliber.

Cavour, who had maintained a watchful eye on the entire course of events, returned to find all of the problems he had left behind in those months.

France called for the consignment of Nice and the Savoy region that he had obstinately denied was part of the agreement. Count Camillo Benso spread a series of lies in an attempt to protect the diplomacy he had implemented. He begged England[11] to help him keep those territories. In the end, he was forced to give in after one more small (small?) subterfuge.

When he ran for election, he propagandized the territorial integrity of Nice and Savoy as part of Piedmont. He won by a landslide and, as soon as he was instated, went to the Parliament and proposed a document that was in evident contrast with his electoral promises and that had already been signed and put into effect. This was unconstitutional and could be classified as "an act of high treason."[12]

The Chamber of Deputies ratified it but experienced shudders of indignation.

William De La Rive said: "I can see no trace of human emotion in Cavour." The representative of the United States in Turin, John Daniel, stated: "He loves money and while he was dealing with the affairs of the State, he managed to accumulate a large fortune for himself." Brofferio, who represented his opposition in Parliament, stated: "He has no sense of morality and is a briber of politicians. He has an insatiable thirst for money and power."

In the end, Giuseppe Garibaldi publicly launched a vehement speech against the government. He was better with a sword than he was with words but his phrase: "You have made me a foreigner in my own land" had its effect and earned its place in the annals of Italy's history. There was even a (false) rumor that Cavour had died and the "democratic" deputy from Sardinia, Giorgio Asproni wrote a venomous page in his diary. "He was from an aristocratic family and lived a vice-filled life. He was a versatile genius full of zeal, who became cunning due to his worldly experiences. He had no scruples and no moral inhibitions. He was greedy for money and power and was insatiable. His expedients and de-

---

[11] Denis Mack Smith, *Cavour, il grande tessitore dell'unità d'Italia*, cit.
[12] *Ibidem*.

vices had no limitations and he was willing to do anything, even if it was dangerous, so long as it ensured victory over his adversaries and retention of his power. He managed to corrupt the media and fix elections with lunches, handshakes, sweet words, and with large sums of money detracted from the secret service's funds. He deceived the public opinion and for ten years was the arbiter of the country."

Yet in those weeks, federalism came within millimeters of becoming adopted. Once the initial phase of obsessive notions of unification had passed, Cavour, who was certainly not stupid, realized the ill feelings that resulted from the centralization of the government. The improvised "unifiers" were causing damage. On May 26, 1860, Cavour addressed the Chamber of Deputies and agreed to tackle the problem himself. It appeared that he had proposed policies that diverged from the previous ones employed by 180 degrees. "We have found Lombardy to be particularly irritated," he began, "and rightly so because of the manner in which events proceeded in their respect. Over the course of a few weeks, I do not know how many thousands of new laws have been passed in a new country with new employees and with entirely new standards."[13]

These signs were in outward contrast to what was being implemented everywhere else. It appeared as though Milan and Florence might be able to retain some form of autonomy, guaranteed by a deputyship, in other words by the king's appointment of a deputy who would assume a sort of power similar to a head of state.

The government's institutional structure was studied by a "temporary legislation committee" that was instated by the State Council. It was entrusted to Gaspare Finali. There was nothing strange about this and there was nothing difficult to implement. The deputy chosen by the king would govern with the assistance of a

---

[13] Camillo Benso Conte di Cavour, *Discorsi parlamentari* (edited by Adolfo Omodeo, Luigi Russo e Armando Saitta), Florence 1932-1973.

council that would have largely the same function as the Council of Ministers.

Here we must return to a thought that Umberto Bossi expressed when he supported the reasoning behind federalism, he intended that Cavour's original thought needed to be elaborated and implemented. Count Camillo Benso had the right idea, but he stopped midway through: it is the remaining path that is missing which would allow Italy to show immediate advancements.

This is the right moment to highlight the fact that during these same years, Bismarck was also establishing the federal State of Germany. He included the Kaiser, the emperor of the confederacy of kings, each of which had their own territories to govern which can be identified by today's *Landers*. They each maintained their respective governments and parliaments but recognized themselves as part of a larger entity that represented them all in a united manner.

Amidst Cavour's letters, in particular those addressed to the jurist Edwin James, there are numerous passages that praise the decentralized government of England. Count Camillo Benso's phase in which he viewed federalism with an idealistic perspective must therefore be considered authentic. It is this aspect that renders this historical figure modern and positive.

However, his enthusiasm for such amendments departed as quickly as it came. Nothing more was done and the entire peninsula was subjected to the ratification of the La Marmora-Rattazzi Law. Today, Italy is still paying the price for the hasty construction of its State. A system of institutions was adapted to a nation that was put together hastily. The system was borrowed from France, which, however, had a centuries old history of cultural unity.

CHAPTER 8

Missed Opportunities: Goodbye, Federalism...

The speed with which history took its course leeched precious time away from the thought process when it came to making important decisions. What was gained in time was lost in the lack of reflection.

Garibaldi departed from Quarto and landed in Marsala so as to ascend the peninsula up to Naples.[1] The governments of Turin, France, and England, who were always preoccupied attending to the "rights of the people," managed to behave like the three little monkeys: they did not see, they did not hear, and they did not speak.

The annals of the *Risorgimento* remember the Battle of Calata-fimi and that of Volturno as well as the Declaration of Salemi and the siege of Palermo.

The *other* version of history prefers to highlight how the Piedmontese managed to play a game of double-crossing.[2] When the *Mille* soldiers began their mission, Cavour asked Salvatore Pes, the marquis of Villamarina as well as his delegated minister in Naples, for "ten or twelve copies of a topographical map of Siciliy in four sheets and twelve copies of that of the Kingdom of the Two Sicilies." He wanted the editions that had been printed by Zenoni "or, if this was not possible, of another important brand." Villamarina managed to provide the maps even if it found itself obliged to send fewer copies of the maps "so as not to rouse the suspicion of the Bourbon government which found itself faced with an important expense in purchasing these papers that lay in

---

[1] Alfonso Scirocco, *In difesa del Risorgimento*, Bologna 1998.
[2] Gigi di Fiore, *Controstoria dell'unità d'Italia: fatti e misfatti del Risorgimento,* Milan 2007.

boxes in the Office of Topography."[3] Certainly the supporters of Garibaldi would have met with little success had it not been for the decision of the Bourbon officials to drop their swords to pick up the sacks of bribe money. On the whole, they could be considered more like thieves than heroes. The theft, embezzlement, and squandering became a commonplace occurrence. Even the incorruptible Mazzini demanded bribe money and sent one of his men to ask for it. It wasn't for him, you understand..." but to establish the financial base for the political party" that needed to buy and finance newspapers, purchase weapons, and invest in full-time revolutionaries.

Thus Italy was born: the grandmother of our country that maintained, and in some cases amplified, the defects of its origins. Those who supported the Unification were not exactly sure how it all came to pass and they had no idea how to manage the fact that such a cast territory had fallen into their hands.

The annexed regions that were aware of what had happened requested that they be allowed administrative autonomy that had been promised to them from the very beginning. Instead, as the discussions proceeded in the Parliament, the notion of federalism became more and more distant, even if, or perhaps even because, it was the most logical solution.

The former Piedmontese political system had been regulated by the Statute of 1848 and had been hastily promulgated by Charles Albert with a centralized government. It consisted of an all-powerful prefect in each province and a mayor nominated by each town. Could an entire country be placed in such a binding suit of armor without even considering local traditions and customs?

Sicily had been a region that possessed a long historical tradition of autonomous government that dated back to the Normans. The moderate liberals of the island had warned that a pure and simple annexation would not be understood by the people. The

---

[3] *La liberazione del Mezzogiorno e la formazione del Regno d'Italia,* Bologna 1962. The letter Cavour wrote to Marqui Pes of Villamarina was dated "Turin, April 25, 1860."

annexation would constitute a risk for a structure that was still in its infancy stage. They proceeded to propose the establishment of an assembly of representatives that would have catered to the pride of the locals. The elected deputies would have, undoubtedly, voted to "fuse" with Piedmont but in conjunction with their assembly in place to address matters strictly pertinent to Sicily.

Naples offered the same reasoning. There were no inclinations towards independence like there were in Palermo. However, Naples remained the capital of a kingdom and providing it with a significant role in the administrative government of the State also meant involving it in the responsibility it would share with the new political entity on the horizon.

Besides, this only entailed keeping a promise that was explicitly made and upon which the Southern patriots were counting.

For Sicily, Cavour had already spoken about self-government and the plebiscite viewed him favorably for this.[4]

On the eve of the elections for the Chamber of Deputies (which was scheduled to meet for the first time on February 18, 1861) Count Camillo Benso ordered that reports be issued stating that the government would take care to ensure the region's administrative autonomy. However, the outcome was quite different.

Carlo Cattaneo and Giuseppe Ferrari, who both boasted patriotic pedigrees and feared no rivals, warned the Southerners.

"Look, they are teasing you ... they had also promised Milan that things would have been handled in a certain manner, but they spoke with a forked tongue. As soon as the opportunity arose, they tore up the projects that they had planned together and proceeded to do things their own way....."[5]

Effectively, even though Cavour continued to speak about federalism, in the obvious attempt to gain more votes, he did not even make an attempt to implement that project.

It is said that Camillo Benso's second term was determined by the reports issued by his correspondents from the South. Farini,

---

[4] Denis Mack Smith, *Cavour, il grande tessitore dell'unità d'Italia*, cit.
[5] Romano Bracalini, *Cattaneo, un federalista per gli italiani*, Milan 1995.

Cassini, Montezemolo, Nigra, Pallavicini all had roles in the temporary governments of the South. They described those lands as a sort of "Affrica," with two f's, that was populated by uncivilized tribes that had no honor and no ideals.

A great deal of credit is due to those native Neapolitans and Sicilians, who had been exiled, for attributing an image of absolute corruption to the South.

Giuseppe La Farina, after having contributed a great deal to the mission of the *Mille* soldiers, openly excluded a return to his native city, Messina. Yet he had been quite nostalgic during his years of voluntary exile.

Giuseppe Massari, however, was even worse. He considered Naples (the city where he was born) to be "ruinous for Italy" and branded his homeland with infamy. According to him, it was a region that was "corrupt, vile, and lacking in that firm virtue that characterizes Piedmont and of that common sense that was native to Tuscany." He offered this comparison: "Believe me ... Naples is worse than Milan."[6]

The Count of Saint Jurioz believed that the Southerners were "born in Italy but might as well have belonged to the *Noveri*, *Dinka*, or *Pulo-Penango* tribes."[7]

The Piedmontese seemed to agree with these notions. Costanza D'Azeglio (whose quote exemplifies the mood of that time period) wrote to her son Emanuele: "No one here wants to annex Naples for reasons that only the Piedmontese can understand." Southerners seemed to be too "distant," or even worse, dangerous, "like marrying a corpse."[8]

Who knows why, if effectively this opinion was widely adopted, Turin accepted to conquer the South. Why did the Southerners who emigrated to the North not state how counterproductive it would be to descend to the "lower" half of Italy?

---

[6] Giuseppe Massari, *Lettere politiche*, cit.
[7] Alessandro Bianco di Saint Jurioz, *Il brigantaggio alla frontier pontificia dal 1869 al 1863*, Milan 1876.
[8] Maria Costa Cardol, *Ingovernabili da Torino. I tormentati esordi dell'unità d'Italia*, Milan 1989.

In 1861, they were afraid that an autonomist constitution would allow an entire land to be vulnerable to gangs of swindlers that only preoccupied themselves with stealing and dealing with their own business. Federalism was boycotted and, along with the centralized government, they wound up being the thieves.

There was time for one more attempt at the institutional level and the opportunity was offered to the good will of Marco Minghetti. He was a minister that came from Emilia Romagna and he believed in the new State that was taking shape but he also took into consideration the needs of his homeland. He elaborated a proposal that was capable of joining the existence of the State with his own decentralized administration.

Each large province of the time (which are the regions today) was endowed with legislative power and financial autonomy with regards to public works, education, healthcare, charitable works, and agriculture. The State was supposed to manage foreign policy, military defense, large public works that were destined for use in all of the territory (railways, postal service, bridges), and was also supposed to keep a watchful eye and regulate the local authorities.

It was a modern project that was almost futuristic.[9] A different Italy would have been born and it certainly would have been a better one. Today, the country takes responsibility for implementing policies that were clearly lacking in any common sense and for the hasty way that its institutions were organized and established.

All of this was a wasted effort: after a long debate, Parliament definitively halted this project. The Council of Ministers did not feel like erasing a proposal that came straight from the heart of the annexed regions and therefore decided to "temporarily" cast it to the side. As often happens in Italy, nothing becomes more definitively established than what was originally intended to be temporary.

---

[9] Marco Minghetti, *I miei ricordi*, Turin 1888.

The Piedmontese laws were quickly enforced on a wide scale. The orders were given even before the Parliament convened and therefore before they could even discuss the matter. The promulgation occurred rapidly. During the night, fifty-three laws that radically modified the institutional structures that were in place were printed in Naples. These new offices were assigned duties that they were incapable of carrying out because of the novelty of the concepts therein.

The true revolution was not the one that Garibaldi spearheaded, but rather the earthquake that occurred in the country's bureaucracy. In an instant, the administration of the country changed drastically. The entire country was forced to deal with law codes that they were unfamiliar with, a scholastic system that was established by the North, a new currency, and a new system of weights and measures. The old one could no longer be used and it was dangerous to even consider using it. The new system, however, had not been divulged yet. The entire country was placed in "stand-by" mode.

The noblest principle to come out of the *Risorgimento* was the self-denomination of the people. If this self-determination was ignored, or even violently erased, where did the reasons for conducting the *Risorgimento* go?

An exaggerated number of officials were sent from Turin whose mission was to dismantle the various committees that had been established in the South. The so-called liberation of Italy was turning into the "Piedmontization" of Italy. However, in this manner, Piedmont only managed to ruin itself and dragged the entire country down with it. The Law of Cretin Supremacy (according to which each person manages to occupy the first hierarchical position that they are inadequate to manage and proceeds to inflict damage from that point onward) took hold on a large scale and was applied with scientific precision. An eager captain from Turin became a pedantic general in Reggio Calabria.[10] A decent teacher

---

[10] Lorenzo Del Boca, *Maledetti Savoia*, Casale Monferrato 1998.

from the North became a terrible scholastic director in the South. A diligent judge in the Savoy capital turned into a boring general prosecutor in a region of the South. The chief of a section found himself promoted to the rank of chief of division and the former chief of division became the prefect.

One could perceive the dissatisfaction in the air. Demonstrations were held in Naples in which the people shouted "Down with Cavour!" They demanded a republic. Even the most motivated liberals felt irritated by the loss of their administrative powers. They had believed the promises of those who had reassured them that they would have the opportunity to establish a few seats of autonomous government that would lay the foundation for a federalist Italy. A few weeks after the Unification of Italy had been officially pronounced, the Duke of Maddaloni passionately complained: "The Piedmontese merchants receive all of the most lucrative supply commissions. The Northern bureaucrats hold almost every public position and they are far more corrupt than their Neapolitan predecessors. The railways are being constructed by Piedmontese workers, who outrageously receive double the salary of the Neapolitans. The porters at the customs checkpoint and the jailers are men from Piedmont. Piedmontese women are hired as wet-nurses in the hospitals almost as if to say that not even the milk of this population is healthy. Is this unity?"[11]

Anything was better than what was actually happening. It would have been better to have Garibaldi, who was all action and no brain…. Mazzini was better too, with all brains and no common sense … even better still were the Bourbon, who were "bourbonic" by definition….

Parliament had neither the time nor the desire to continue discussing the notion of introducing a federalist system. The question was simply put aside and never spoken about again. It was a subject that did not loan itself to the theatrical style of rhetoric that the deputies employed at that time. The problem was too serious to

---

[11] *Atti parlamentari*, 1861.

kindle the fire in the hearts of the patriots. It was a much better idea to chase the moods of those who requested the completion of the Unification by conquering Venice and Rome. This was a notion that had more criminal aspects than abstruse ones. To seize Venice, it would be necessary to clash with Austria, who could not wait to break our bones. To seize Rome, it would be necessary to clash with France, who would have taken back all of the gifts they had given us in the Second War of Independence.

Yet the ministers and deputies wasted hours, days, and months describing what was, according to them, the "nation's opinion" which in reality was just the product of manipulated enthusiasm. They did so even if it meant that they made themselves and their country vulnerable to a bad reputation in the eyes of the rest of the world. Federico Sclopis commented: "Our national patriotism does not manifest itself in the form of perseverance but rather in intermittent shudders." Venice.... Rome....

In Florence, a statue of Dante Alighieri was inaugurated and he was draped with the tricolor flag. In accordance with the anti-clerical standards of the State, there were no masses or blessings given. The patriotic priest recruited Dante and made him a precursor of the Italian Unification. It appeared, to the orator, that the statue of Dante indicated the path that the king (who was present) should take and that he was saying, "Cesare ... why don't you accompany me?" Massimo D'Azeglio joked about a Dante that was a supporter of Garibaldi. Niccolò Tommaso, who despite being a patriot was not stupid, manipulated a well-known quote from the Divine Comedy: *"Farti non puoi più parti da te stesso/poiché in mezzo ai politici t'han messo"* (You no longer belong to yourself because they have placed you amongst politicians).

The Italian Parliamentary sessions always began by paying homage to literature or science. The president would announce that a deputy had donated to the Chamber their latest work. Occasionally, the works were useful but since the majority of the deputies were failed writers and artists, trivial pettifogs with graphomaniacal tendencies; the Parliament library was filled with boring, prolix books.

These sessions lasted between nine and ten hours at a time and concluded nothing. Hours were spent discussing trivial details. The more serious matters were resolved in an instant, at the end of the session, when everyone was exhausted. The Parliament would surrender like a small town under siege because by this time its members were tired and hungry. This is when the bad habits manifested themselves.

In the 1800s, it seemed that the Italian language was coined for the use of lofty rhetoric. It is not even a close relative of the Italian that is spoken today. Even French, English, and Spanish have changed in the past 150 years but not in the same manner that Italian has. At that time, the Italian language was closer to the sweeter "new style" than the modern one. To say "shortly after" they said "a short while ago"; to warn about danger, they said: "one must run the risk"; and if they had to express a vote that was unfavorable to something, they said: "my spirit is ill-suited to these theories." Venice…. Rome….

The theme of the Unification lent itself particularly to that prolix style of speech adopted by the Fathers of Our Country. The Parliament presented motions, approved them, and voted to enact them. The town squares were filled with people that collected money and clothing to prepare for a new mission for the *Mille* soldiers.

Each institution, no matter how provincial, issued patriotic writings to be diffused amongst themselves.

The revolutionary din transferred itself within the administrative entities. The officials did not know whether to apply the laws that had expired or the new ones that arrived from Turin which were often in direct contrast to each other. New laws always need to undergo a trial period first.

Confusion turned to fear that the bureaucrats, who had been hired for political merit, incited in their colleagues, who up until that point had worked at a desk below an image of a duke, grand duke, or the Bourbon king. The blue-blooded patriots were subjected to constant scrutiny.

Cesare Cantù had been to jail because the Austrians had considered him too restless in regards to political matters. His observations remain well above any suspicion: "The clever men who were able to desert in time and declare themselves victims, tend to make others forget their previous actions by exaggerating newer ones, which include denouncing, slandering, and taking vile pleasure in mortifying good citizens. The same characters passed from city to city and region to region inciting the people to applaud or launch imprecations, thereby ensuring that Italy would be composed of people who did not ask questions, but expressed love and submission to it. We found ourselves numerous people who were ready to denounce anyone in papers and clubs. They were the very same people who reported us to the Austrian police. The newspapers are ready to satisfy a public that is hungry for scandals and rhetorical speeches. They offer no precise information but rather adhere to the whims of the partisans when they exaggerate their superficial and passionate speeches that test the limits of good manners. They created false virtues and berated anyone who did not conform to their thoughts by calling them reactionaries, clericalists, supporter of Austria, Bourbonic."[12]

What was the result? "The heads of office do not dare request that their subordinates actually carry out their assigned duties because they fear being reported to the newspapers. It is pointless to even proceed with a lawsuit because the magistrate is also afraid of public opinion (in other words, of the newspapers) particularly the humoristic ones that aimed to injure reputations more than inspire laughter. In the midst of all of these presumed scandals, with which one could ruin the reputation of many influential, though inconveniently positioned, men, real scandals erupted. No one dared to speak of those."[13]

The North was disappointed and irritated. The South was rebellious and violent.

There were many difficulties to face and even if one chose to deal with them, it would be difficult to improve the situation. The most concrete matters, however, were hardly given any real play.

---

[12] Cesare Cantù, *Il cimitero dell'Ottocento*, Milan 1954.
[13] *Ibidem.*

The praetors of the demagogy imposed this Unitarian State: a single blanket needed to cover the industries of Como, the farms in Romagna, the association of San Leucio, and the workers in Aspromonte. It also needed to cover the refined, aspirated Italian spoken in Tuscany, the French-inspired Italian spoken in Turin, the Neapolitan version of Italian along with all of its lexical facets that define the character of each individual, and the drawl that is present in Bologna.

The notion that a centralized form of power was to be employed became evident when Victor Emanuel remained II (the second). For Ricasoli, this was the confirmation that the regions had not been united but rather had been annexed.

"When the Council of Ministers evaluated the various proposals, Victor Emanuel, with a steady voice declared that he did not offer his consent should they decide to change the dynastic order because, in his opinion, it seemed ungrateful towards his glorious ancestors who, with their wisdom and their swords, had left him the crown that rested upon his head."[14]

He was Victor Emanuel II and he wanted to remain known as Victor Emanuel II. Anyone who expected a sign, even a small one, that the mentality of the tiny Savoy country had finally been abandoned, was left disappointed.

The new title was the subject of many a debate held in private meetings, in the Senate and House of Deputies, in the newspapers, amongst the more influential deputies before it was finally presented to the Parliament. Cavour supported his king's reasoning and boycotted the proposal of Lorenzo Valeria to give Victor Emanuel the title of "King of the Italians." That was unsuitable as well.

It seemed paradoxical that a State should ask the international community to recognize its status by reciprocally accepting foreign diplomatic delegations, yet their head was already considered "second."

---

[14] Giuseppe Massari, *Vittorio Emanuele II*, Milan 1912.

The truth of the matter was that Italy was no longer well liked and even those who had contributed to its creation found themselves dealing with a legal nightmare.

Even the members of high society were skeptical.

The *Gazzetta del Popolo* informed its readers that every Wednesday, "Countess A. from M." opened her luxurious apartment to "many illustrious celebrities of the political and literary world."[15] Conversations were held at the beginning of the evening and a ball was held at eleven o'clock. Performances were held by "Mister Galliano with his strange xylophone composed of glasses with varying shapes and sizes laid out in a crate. By lightly rubbing his fingers along the rims of the glasses it is possible to play any musical piece." There were many enthusiastic and patriotic comments made concerning the decision to making Italian the official language of the reception. It was a brave decision. The newspaper encouraged all of the other ladies of high society to copy this initiative. Only forty ladies volunteered. All of the others continued to speak French because it was the language they were most familiar with.

Perhaps it was for that reason that in the South, even in the most "Italian" environments, such as the one headed by Benedetto Croce, the people wound up supporting the philosophical theories of idealism. Due to the fact that they came from Germany, they drew up a declaration of independence from France and therefore delivered a slap in the face of Piedmont, who continued to adopt Paris's cultural models.

The roads of patriotism and of its "patriotic" dissent are infinite.

---

[15] Vittorio Bersezio, Appendix of "La Gazzetta del Popolo," February-March 1861.

Chapter 9

The Public Debt that Currently Strangles Us Is Due to the 150th Anniversary of the Italian Unification

The number that comprises the Italian public debt is complicated to read and to comprehend especially if one is not a specialist in the respective field. Everyone, however, understands that it is an enormous burden that makes it difficult for the country to "run." It even makes it difficult to walk.

During the course of the 16th Legislature, a law was passed concerning the State's accounting and budget. This legislative measure was passed with a nearly unanimous vote even though the media, which are generally more concerned with reporting gossip, only absentmindedly reported this detail. Numbers are boring by definition. It is boring to preoccupy oneself with accounting and the balancing of budgets.

The law states that there needs to be communication between the accounting systems and the budget balance. Basically, public entities need to communicate amongst themselves using predefined algebraic terms. It is not possible that a township could receive financial assistance from the province, region, and the State and that none of these entities is aware that the other has already assisted this town.

Yet this is exactly what used to happen....

In the past, a style of logic took the country by storm and benefitted a certain political class that, instead of governing, wound up specializing itself in accumulating public funds.

The new law disciplines the entire planning process: first the report on the economy and public finance must be presented by April 15th, the decisions made by public finance must be presented by September 15th, and the bill for the stability law must be presented by October 15th along with the bill establishing the State budget. These must all be followed by the bills that are linked to the public finance maneuver and the update to the stability project which are to be presented to the European Union and the European Commission.

Expenses must be planned and there will be strict monitoring by the European community. The maximum cost of public employment will need to be delineated. This law puts a stop to the constant blitzes that resulted in the increase of the salaries of public employees. This increase highlighted the disparity between the salaries in the public and private sectors as it became evident that both were not treated objectively. The private sector is already considered to be at a disadvantage because their jobs are not guaranteed the same stability as in the public sector.

This mentality of "milking" the government has been prevalent for years. It is this very mentality that has transformed the public employment sector into a giant buffer for social security. This of course damaged the true social security system for those who really needed it. Public administration found itself carrying a tremendous amount of dead weight. Things can only improve in the future, even though it will be necessary to first bring the debt to levels that are compatible with the development of the country and its productive capacity. Sacrifices will be necessary.

The country is in dire need of infrastructures, public works, technological upgrades, and in these hard financial times, the country must also invest in initiatives that support the business world. But how does one go about spending money that one does not have?

We have lived above our means and we must now lower our expectations and plan on saving our resources. The few resources that we have left must be carefully allotted using a stringent criterion of prioritization.

Universities certainly deserve attention but if there are dozens of degree programs with one student, would it be such a scandal to ask that student to exercise his imagination a bit more and attend some classes with a few fellow students?

If it is not possible to quickly finance works that are in dire need of assistance, it will be pointless to complain if in Pompei, three meters worth of ancient walls collapse because it was not possible to repair them in time. These controversies become sterile and even criminal if they are sidelined out of a spitefully adopted political principle. In the year of the Jubilee, Rome was under the administration of Mayor Francesco Rutelli when a piece of the Aurelian Wall crumbled. The damage was equivalent to nineteen times the amount of damage to the House of the Gladiators in Pompei. Did anyone protest? Who asked for the rectification of this damage? Is there a way to request the resignation of the person or, in case the interested person was not able to instantaneously disappear, to fire them through the vote of some assembly?

More recently, a wing of the fortress in Sestola, located in the province of Modena, collapsed.[1] One of the surrounding walls of the castle of Montecucco also crumbled in the same area near Modena. This is even more serious because 10 million Euro had just been spent for their restoration.

Were there any investigations conducted? Questions asked? Clarity?

The "hole" in our State budget comes from far back and the *Risorgimento* cannot exempt itself from taking its responsibility in this.

In the thirty-four years between the fall of the kingdom of Napoleon Bonaparte and the First War of Independence, Piedmont could have boasted a solid administration. In the twelve years following 1848, during the "period of preparation," the deficit was over one billion: 1,024,970,595 Piedmontese lira (at the time).

The first blow that the State budget took came from its defeat in the First War of Independence.

War, everywhere, costs a tremendous amount of money. On top of the expenses that the country had to normally face, it be-

---

[1] "Le Pompei democratiche. Crolla un altro castello in Emilia ma nel Pd nessuno si dimette. Dopo la rocca di Sestola, cede la cinta di Montecuccolo," *Il Resto del Carlino*, January 4 2011.

came necessary to repair the damages inflicted by Austria. Initially, Vienna requested 250 million in damages, which was an amount
that was entirely disproportionate with respect to Piedmont's financial means. They settled upon 75 million.[2] In order to honor
this amount promised, it was necessary to call upon international
banks to provide an advancement of capital. We managed to receive a loan of 315 million.

The negotiations happened at the same time the merger between the Bank of Turin and the Bank of Genoa occurred, in a context laden with conflicts of interest that are quite unclear.[3] The
Ministers who handled the operation along with Count Cavour
who, although he was no longer part of the government became
involved because of certain friendships he had maintained, were
accused of having usurped legislative power. Their only intention
was to establish a banking policy that benefitted only a few financial groups.

The various aspects of the scandal were reported by the "*La
Concordia*" newspaper, according to which Cavour had received
"at least one hundred and fifty thousand lira" as did: the Nigra
brothers, Count Salmour, and the bankers Defernex and Bolmida.[4]
How embarrassing.

Even the periodical *L'Armonia* criticized the methods that public finance employed at that time. "The Minister asks for loans and
plans to set new taxes. The Chamber of Deputies discusses these
tax reforms, votes and approves them. The citizens pay." The
newspaper was not stingy with even the most ferocious comments: "We will examine," wrote the editor, "our finances in this
state of absolutism and compare them to those in the state of freedom." The comparison was entirely impossible to conduct. "The
rule of absolutist governments consisted in spending less than
what was collected. There were not as many chairs for professors
and economists but in compensation, there was more money in

---

[2] Cesare Spellanzon – Ennio di Nolfo, *Storia del Risorgimento*, Milan 1933-1965.
[3] Adriano Viarengo, *op. cit.*
[4] *Ibidem.*

the bank." In 1847, the credit balance was around 41 million that initially turned into a small "hole" in the budget and then became an enormous chasm. "In six years, from 1848 to 1854, we were issued loans in the amount of 503,252,161 lira with an increase due to passive interest rates of 28,901,443 that needed to be paid to the lenders." Our finance policies were quite jolly and distracted. "We had a debt of 503 million but only 418 million ever made it to the State's coffers. In other words, 85 million evaporated. Whoever managed to get their hands on those millions (and someone must have gotten their hands on them because they never made into the public funds) is right to side with the loan system!"[5]

The "evaporation" to which the newspaper referred to did not necessarily imply theft, or at least not exclusively. The money evaporated because the banks considered it risky to loan Turin money and they safeguarded themselves by imposing a considerable sum of money to be paid in advance as a sort of insurance.

The new State had little trust: the loan contractors had to be flattened under the high interest rates. Out of 100 that had been loaned, 82-83 made it to public funds but when the budgets needed to be balanced, the entire sum had to be paid.

In Italy, no one was inspired to undertake any business ventures because it was easier to make money by purchasing treasury bonds. Those who grew wealthy between 1860 and 1870 did so without producing goods and therefore did not increase the country's production either.

In compensation, they were not timid when the time came to put their hands in the pockets of the vast majority of the remaining citizens.

In the meantime, Cavour became the Minister of Finance and he was certainly not afraid of the word "taxes" especially if it meant that others had to pay them. He believed that the imposition of a progressive tax was completely unacceptable. He was amongst the wealthiest men in all of Piedmont. How could he allow the

---

[5] *L'Armonia*, November 20, 1855.

State to put its hands in his own pockets by his own doing? However, he did not hesitate to introduce new taxes and managed to resurrect taxes that had been introduced by Napoleon Bonaparte and abolished during the French Restoration.[6] He thought to implement taxes that were different from the land taxes: industrial and professional. Today, this would be considered conducting a study on different sectors.

The resulting revenue was not sufficient and it was necessary once again to knock on the doors of other banks.

Cavour established a mortgage loan that was worth 75 million that was guaranteed by the sub-Alpine railways (which were an entity managed by the State) with the assistance of Alexandre Lombard from the Oldier and Lombard Bank of Geneva and that of Emilio and Ippolito De La Rue. The discussion held with the London banker Carl Joachim Hambro was exhausting, but in the end, they all signed. The amount was not entirely satisfactory. Initially, they had proposed an interest rate of 90, but then they decreased it to 86-87, but were forced to accept 85.[7]

How to go about increasing the revenue? The Parliament organized itself so as to make the Church pay. The Siccardi laws were passed and they included the expropriation of convents and the confiscated goods would go to the State. That small, confiscated treasure was supposed to be placed into a fund whose administration was to be determined by a law to be signed by Urbano Rattazzi. Who was appointed to manage this fund? Rattazzi's brother.[8]

Luigi Fransoni, the Archibishop of Turin, gave the order to protest these laws and was promptly arrested. The extremely pious Count of Santa Rosa was refused his Last Rites upon his death bed because he had voted in favor of the laws that targeted the Church and did not ask for forgiveness. The archibishop, who was held responsible, was exiled and his possessions were confiscated.

---

[6] Italo de Feo, *Cavour, l'uomo e l'opera*, Milan 1969.
[7] Carlo Maria Franzero, *Il conte di Cavour e i suoi banchieri inglesi*, Turin 1968.
[8] Adriano Viarengo, *op. cit.*

The Pope refused to name his successor. A dozen years later, the archbishop died in exile.

It goes without saying that the Church's confiscated goods, which were put up for auction, wound up benefitting a few members of the world of finance who simply grew wealthier. Piedmont's budget merely contained crumbs that were far too insufficient to fuel the administration.

It became necessary to negotiate another international loan. This time, Baron Rothschild contracted a loan of 66 million. To recuperate, taxes were imposed on alcoholic beverages.

Yet another loan was required to finance the Crimean War.

Cavour decided that 25 million would suffice. The English believed that that amount was significantly more than what was necessary. In October, Cavour had to ask for another 25 million. In December, while on another visit to Great Britain, he asked for 25 million for a third time.

Piedmont was becoming a bottomless pit thanks to its expansionistic ambitions.

Since they predicted that the Second War of Independence was about to take place, they were forced to request other loans: first 40 million then 150. The Chamber of Deputies voted with near unanimity and there were only 23 contrary votes.[9]

We barely had enough time to take a breath when we yet again found ourselves having to ask for more money. Garibaldi had just "conquered" the Kingdom of the Two Sicilies and needed to pay for it.

The Red Shirts were, for the most part, anti-clerical. However, the Church notion they had the least respect for was the 7th Commandment: Thou shalt not steal.

"The ease with which they withdrew funds from public funds to gratify their supporters and friends prompts us to reflect upon the management of finances during the dictatorship. We are speaking about enormous amounts of money that were managed

---

[9] *Atti parlamentari,* 1854-1855.

in a completely autonomous fashion and that were never properly accounted for. A significant portion of the Bourbon silver lay in the coffers of the Kingdom of Naples. Traces of the millions of ducats worth of silver were lost."[10] Large sums of money were deposited between Naples and Sicily and these funds made their way to the North as well as France and England through the chartering and acquisition of maritime goods, weapons, and clothing. Or perhaps they were just lost along the way. Sixty thousand coats were purchased for twenty-one thousand soldiers. The difference was immediately sold on the black market. Many Garibaldi supporters left in miserable conditions and returned home with pockets full of money. That which was not stolen was destroyed by negligence and carelessness.

The historian Roberto Martucci managed to estimate the value of the spoils: half a billion Piedmontese lira of the time.[11] This amount is equivalent to the future public debt of unified Italy. It is nine times the debt that was contracted to participate in the Crimean War.

Cavour used official funds as well as secret ones to bribe the officials of the Bourbon army as well as the Navy's admirals. He spent, and forced others to spend, exaggerated sums of money to fund "proclamations" in favor of Victor Emanuel II that were never made.

A man named Goritte,[12] a lawyer, appeared before Farini during the siege of Gaeta claiming that he could convince the King of the Two Sicilies to surrender. In exchange, he expected them to return a portion of the treasures that the King had left behind in Naples. This was highly improbable given that Francis II had left his palace showing a complete disregard for the money he left behind. If he had only desired it, he could have asked the bank. Count Cavour, ever informed, quickly gave his consent: "Bridges of gold to Francis II! The fall of Gaeta is too priceless to pass up."

[10] Roberto Martucci, *L'invenzione dell'Italia unita 1855-1864*, Milan 1999.
[11] *Ibidem*.
[12] Pier Augusto Jaeger, *Francesco II di Borbone, l'ultino re di Napoli*, Milan 1982.

Goritte received a good amount of funds under the table. He spent this money without accomplishing anything and presented himself before them yet again asking for more money. This time the Piedmontese did not fall for his tricks, even when Goritte invented explanations excuses, forced himself to justify his "beggar's" diplomacy, and attempted to obtain some sort of compensation for expenses he had already incurred. At the end of the war, he felt morally inclined to explain himself by putting everything in writing. He began to write a book, which he temporarily called *"Political Effort to Cede Gaeta in December of 1860 without Further Loss of Blood."* This is exactly what everyone wanted to know more about.

Unfortunately, the author maintained that his story would not be properly comprehended without an introduction that addressed the issue in a more general manner. In his sort of preface, he began to narrate the history of the Bourbon dynasty from the Restoration. This introduction became quite lengthy and addressed complex dynastic issues. It wound up comprising two enormous tomes of some thousand pages and weighed several kilograms. He did not live long enough to complete his literary masterpiece and therefore was never quite able to explain what exactly he and the Piedmontese had managed to accomplish underneath the bastions of Gaeta. There were only trace mentions of the hoax.

What infamous pages! The incorruptible Mazzini requested bribe money for the work that needed to be done on the railways.[13] He justified his request: "Where others would take their share from each business, I intend to fortify the coffers of the party...."

Agostino Bertani withdrew enormous sums of money to fund the Republican Left Party at that time.[14]

Scialoja, who was sent hastily by Cavour to keep an eye on Garibaldi's actions, exclaimed: "What....? Do you intend to make millions[15] disappear so that all that is left is the Unification....?"

---

[13] Vito Di Dario, *Oh Mia Patria! 1861, un inviato speciale nel primo anno d'Italia*, Milan 1990.
[14] Roberto Martucci, *L'invenzione dell'Italia unita 1855-1864*, cit.

Ippolito Nievo[16] was one of the cashiers of the expedition and was perhaps the only honest one. He had managed to keep all of the accounts and balances in order. When word got out that in the South, too much was being stolen; he chose to defend his honor. He sent a telegram to Turin stating that he would return with all of the documents necessary to demonstrate his efficiency. He boarded the steamboat *Ercole* but never arrived at his destination. They realized that the steamboat was late after a week went by. Only then was a search conducted. Anyone who believes that the State[17] was behind his death has reason to spare.

Poor government seemed to know no limitations ... distribution of official titles so that 3 or 4 people were hired to carry out the job of one person (which clearly none of the four accomplished) ... recruitment of men known for their corruption ... robbery and bribery regarding the supply of just about everything ... the squandering of public funds to buy almost anything including ships...

When the sums were counted[18], the Minister of the Treasury, Pietro Bastogi, revealed that the "hole" in the budget had reached 2 billion and 402 million. Piedmont's debt accounted for 55% of the total and it was composed largely of the expenses it incurred for the Unification of Italy.

Public spending amounted to 900 million and a large part of that was due to the amount invested in weapons and maintaining the army. The first financial maneuver was to request a loan for 500 million. From that moment onward the deficit continued to be covered by a massive amount of debt. When Rome was conquered, which was the moment in which the Unification of Italy was considered complete; those 2 billion had become 9.[19]

There was nothing left. Taxes were the only things that were available in copious amounts. They varied from 42% to 48% and a

---

[15] *Ibidem.*
[16] Dario Mantovani, *Ippolito Nievo, il poeta soldato,* Milan 1899.
[17] Stanislao Nievo, *Il prato in fondo al mare,* Milan 1974.
[18] Francesco Saverio Nitti, *Il bilancio dello Sato dal 1862 al 1896-1897,* Bari 1958.
[19] *Ibidem.*

tax was placed on ground meat. There was even a tax that needed to be paid according to the size of one's windows. People paid taxes to eat ... and breathe.

They deceived themselves into thinking that they could pay off the debt "by stealing the people's bread by taxing the 600 lira of income they had. In the meantime, they allowed their prefects the privilege of promotion and entertainment expenses that, during important holidays or other occurrences, they used to throw aristocratic balls. The aristocrats can dance very well in their own homes...."[20]

Any effort to halt this "merry" approach to finance failed. When Minister Quintino Sella proposed to establish rules to ensure that the administration run smoothly he was criticized by Francesco Crispi: "If you propose these reforms then that means that you are a man with no principles!"

Giacinto de Sivo,[21] a supporter of the Bourbon dynasty to his very core, commented: "In five years' time, the taxes tripled but the land did not triple its fruits. In only two years, the Unification of Italy managed to ruin 2000 men in Basilicata. Naples, who was fortunate enough to not have known the Vandals, however, came to know Garibaldi instead."

Even those who supported the other side could not express themselves differently.

The French diplomat Henry D'Ideville, a former admirer of Cavour, was forced to accept that "the Italian Unification generated boldness, the war against religion, compulsory loans, and income taxes along with the most significant amount of taxes, direct and indirect, ever imposed. This condemned the State to bankruptcy, lack of religion, and chaos. Confederacy would have been the ideal conservative solution to the Italian problem. I don't believe that there is not a single Italian that loves his country that would not embrace this solution."[22]

---

[20] Carlo Dossi, *Note azure*, Milan 1964.
[21] Giacinto De Sivo, *Storia delle Due Sicilie dal 1847 al 1861*, Rome 1863-1864.
[22] Henry D'Ideville (edited by Guido Artom), *op. cit.*

Patrick O'Clery[23] calculated that in 1866 a former inhabitant of the Kingdom of the Two Sicilies paid 28 francs in taxes, which was double the amount they spent before the "liberation." The other states wound up in worse conditions. Take the Veneto region as an example. With the declaration of the Unified State, their economy was destroyed and an omnivorous, spiteful bureaucracy ruined the lives of farmers and small business owners. They paid the Hapsburgs 11 lira and the Italian-Savoys 31 lira.

In this disgrace common to all Italians, there was at least one difference. While the Southerners theoretically only had to pay taxes, they did not think twice when it came time to evade them. The Venetians and the North had to pay them … and they did.

---

[23] Patrick Keyes O'Clery, *La rivoluzione italiana: come fu fatta l'unità della nazione*, Milan 2000.

CHAPTER 10

A New Government Every 100 Days and the Ills of Political Instability

A long with the public debt, political instability explains the lack of competitiveness of a country. Before bills can become laws, they must go through a planning and elaborating stage. If after every few months, the ministers are replaced, this process slows down because it is necessary for the ministers to familiarize themselves with their new surroundings, staff, and the task at hand. As soon as they are ready to begin their job ... it is time to change!

In this regard, the *Risorgimento* and the Republic are practically the same, even from the statistical perspective. The average life of an administration was six months.

We began with Cesare Balbo, Count of Vinadio, who was personally chosen by Charles Albert. He made this decision without any forewarning. The Savoy king, in the previous years, had waffled in between liberal uprisings. This was the product of his Parisian education and of his loyalty to absolutist monarchy. In his youth, he was more liberal than conservative, though when he grew older, the situation reversed. During the revolt of 1821, he had openly supported the *Carbonari* that demanded a constitution. However, he would have had to endure the hostility of Carlo Felice, who would have treated him as though he were a traitor to the monarchy. He sent Felice to Tuscany to be rid of him and for years he harbored the idea of not choosing him as his successor to the throne.

Charles Albert forced himself to undergo a sort of crash course in conservative doctrines. He fought alongside the Spanish reactionaries and maintained correspondence with the most bigoted sovereigns. He attempted to pass himself off as the champion of conservatives.[1]

Nonetheless, to assure himself the throne, he was forced to solemnly swear that his kingdom would remain as it had been given to him. For about fifteen years he was actually quite zealous about respecting this oath.

Then 1848 came about, and Europe was ablaze with insurrections. The kings, due to pressures from the mobs, began to allow for some constitutional reforms. At first, Turin declared that, as far as they were concerned, they would have handled the mobs "Using whatever means necessary."[2]

Charles Albert stood vehemently behind his words: "I am not like that Bourbon monarch that became submissive to the diktat established by the rebels, which is the most deleterious thing that I can imagine." He had sworn that he would maintain his promise at all costs. He continued to repeat that he would have never given in and that if they had wanted him dead, then they could kill him but he would not allow for even the smallest of concessions.

He said this to his friends and to everyone he knew, though it is uncertain if he did so to boost their morale or his own. "My strongest desire," he wrote with his tidy penmanship, "is to fight until the end without conceding anything to the demands of an insurrection."

In the cafés of Piazza San Carlo, around tables crowded with customers, De La Tour narrated a discussion that he had had with the king. "'They want a constitution, but I will never give it to them!' He tapped his snuffbox as he stared me straight in the eyes. Have you understood correctly? I said that he will never give it to them and therefore it is highly likely that he will give them one soon."

In fact, a few hours later, while making a great effort to be heard over the discussions of the crowds that had occupied nearly

---

[1] Silvio Bertoldi, *Il re che tentò di fare l'Italia. Vita di Carlo Alberto di Savoia*, Milan 2000.
[2] Giorgio Falco, *Lo statuto albertino e la sua preparazione*, Rome 1945.

all of the rooms in the palace, the Minister Giacomo Borelli mustered up some courage and told the king that he absolutely needed to sign that document. "You must do so immediately, sire, to avoid that it be imposed upon you." The other ministers were in agreement and they tried to embellish the conversation by offering considerations of various opportunities that would present themselves as a result. They did not realize that Charles Albert was on the verge of having a nervous breakdown.[3]

During that time, the king had problems with his liver and suffered from poor digestion. Each time a problem with his health manifested itself, the doctors practiced the only form of therapy that they knew and could perform successfully: bloodletting. What benefits could be derived by further weakening a man who was already ill remains a mystery. This was the only official form of medicine that was practiced and only on rare occasions did it actually kill the patient. They removed a half-liter of blood on that occasion, left him to cry for ten minutes. Then they heard him scream. Finally, they patiently listened to his declarations in which he announced that he would prefer to abdicate than sign to approve a decision in which he did not believe. He appeared calmer.

He called, one after another, a dozen priests that he trusted.[4] He needed advice and, perhaps, to be assured that his oath of many years ago could actually be less binding than he had initially had perceived. Simple priests were not sufficient, even if they were numerous. The Bishop of Vercelli was called. Due to the vows the Bishop had taken he was considered to be closer to God and therefore could be considered the spokesperson for a higher power. This last discussion reassured him.[5]

Ok! He presented himself before the dignitaries of his court and the men of the government to tell them that he would accept to make this sacrifice.

---

[3] *Ibidem.*
[4] Niccolò Rodolico, *Carlo Alberto negli anni 1843-1849*, Florence 1943.
[5] *Ibidem.*

On March 4, 1848: the decision, which was destined to garner the praises of posterity as a demonstration of an agreement between a monarch and his subjects, was adopted with the same enthusiasm with which one enters an operating room to undergo a delicate operation.

Fine then! He imposed two conditions: that they find a way to make Catholicism the official religion of the State so as to preserve it and strengthen it and that there be no celebrations because an abuse like that to which he had just been subjected were not conducive to singing and dancing.

The first action taken by the new administration was to expel the Jesuits[6] from the Kingdom of Sardinia in an attempt to eliminate their followers who were too close to them. When it became common knowledge that the constitution had been signed, the people took to the streets and surrounded the royal palace and expected Charles Albert to come to the window because they wanted to carry him around the city as a sign of triumph. Even the women participated, a rare occurrence, and they adorned themselves with tricolor bows and scarves that they affixed to their skirts or their hair.

Everyone seemed to encourage a war against Austria and they asked that the army be sent to the border. Even the ministers expressed unanimity regarding this issue, but only because those who vote to go into war are seldom those that fight on the front lines, but rather are the ones who send others to do the fighting.

There were no elections held. The government was formed by a few notable members of the Piedmontese aristocracy. Some even thought that Cavour could have become the Minister of Agriculture. He thought so as well, but was forced to face disappointment.

Balbo admired him. When he founded the newspaper *Il Risorgimento,* he called him to become a member of the editorial staff but had to accept the fact that he was hated by both sides of the

---

[6] Angela Pellicciari, *Risorgimento da riscrivere*, Milan 1998.

government. If Cavour was allowed to speak, the discussion immediately ended because everyone else rose from their seats and left.[7]

That government was temporary by definition. He submitted his resignation even though it was only published on July 6th.

On the 27th of July, the second cabinet was inaugurated. The Prime Minister was the Lombard Gabrio Casati, a major figure in the Five Day Insurrection in Milan. Vincenzo Gioberti was also made a minister with no budget.

The first armistice, which followed the defeat at Custoza, caused this government to be overturned.

Cesare Alfieri was appointed Prime Minister, even though everyone seemed to favor Ottavio Thaon di Revel, a strong figure in the government.

The various political circles and the democrats insisted upon continuing the war. But who would give the orders? The government changed yet again with Vincenzo Gioberti as its Prime Minister who proved to be less audacious than expected. The bellicose project he used as his campaign platform served him well, but only to attain this position of power. Once he sat in the most prestigious seat he figured that he could merely sit back and rest on his laurels.

Each time the Prime Minister changed, so did his entire cabinet. Sometimes, the Prime Minister simply reordered his cabinet anyway.

For example, over the course of twelve months spanning from 1848 to 1849, in between the two defeats of the First War of Independence, the Minister of War, which at that time was the worst ministry to have to manage, passed from Provana of Collegno to Franzini, to Dabormida, to La Marmora, to Chiodo, then back to Dabormida.[8] Each one believed that his predecessor understood nothing and felt the need to undo the laws that his predecessor had implemented and began anew. To emphasize the notion that

---

[7] Denis Mack Smith, *Cavour, il grande tessitore dell'unità d'Italia*, cit.
[8] Piero Pieri, *Storia militare del Risorgimento*, cit.

renewal meant change, pressured by a climate that expected the previous laws be overthrown, Dabormida undid all the laws that he had passed in his previous term.

The disaster provoked by the Battle of Novara brought the Savoy Gabriel De Launay to the position of Prime Minister, though only for a few days because his post was soon assigned to Massimo D'Azeglio. They did not call Cavour this time either and he furiously stormed off to his home in Leri, cursing the destiny of the country and he comforted himself "by living as though that whore known as Italy did not exist."[9]

Charles Albert had abdicated the throne and in his place sat Victor Emanuel II. The hagiography of the *Risorgimento* speaks of his proud attitude. "The Savoy dynasty knows about exile but they do not know anything about dishonor." It is certain that that phrase was never uttered. Furthermore, Victor Emanuel presented himself almost as if he were going to apologize. He challenged his father who, according to him, had made a mistake and blamed the democrats for having led him down the wrong path. He, he assured everyone, would not commit the same error and planned to re-organize Piedmont, who in the meantime had taken too many liberties.

In fact, he proceeded to dissolve the Chamber of Deputies where the Leftist party held considerable power and called for new elections. The results did not comfort him because the democrats maintained their representation and were powerful enough to condition parliamentary decisions.

Victor Emanuel proceeded to dissolve the Chamber again and called for another election,[10] but this time he sent the voters to the ballots with a menacing message: the Moncalieri Proclamation. It basically stated that if the people did not vote the way he believed they should, they could not reserve the right to complain when

---

[9] Adriano Viarengo, *op. cit.* A letter from Camillo Benso di Cavour to Michelangelo Castelli was cited.

[10] Silvio Bertoldi, *Il re che fece l'Italia. Vita di Vittorio Emanuele II di Savoia*, Milan 2002.

things went awry. This was the end of the Statute and he would have resumed governing without a Parliament.

This time the Parliament voted the right way. Last time, Cavour had been outrageously defeated. This time around he was able to gain a seat in the Chamber of Deputies and on August 5th, when the Minister of Agriculture Pietro di Santa Rosa died, he was called to be a part of the government once again.

That ministry suited him. Count Camillo Benso resumed his meddlesome ways and was particularly concerned with issues pertaining to the financial sector. D'Azeglio told his nephew Emanuel: "He was built to conduct business and Parliament, for that matter. However, he is a despot like the devil and I do not love tyrants. It is only a matter of a few days before I will leave my post."[11]

Actually, it was the others who chose to leave first. Every month or so, another minister resigned from his post because he did not agree with Cavour: first came Mameli, then Nigra, followed by Gioia and Siccardi.

Count Camillo was already preparing his cabinet. With a maneuver worthy of a turncoat, he went about plotting modern civilization's first political upset. Who aided him in his effort? Urbano Rattazzi.

The Rattazzis were a family of patriots from the city of Alessandria.[12] One of them had participated in one of the first insurrections that occurred in 1821 and was named political commissioner of his province. Another, Alessandro, lead the revolt in Casale. When Carlo Felice had been restored to power, they were both condemned to death and were not executed only because they were able to flee. They both died in exile. Urbano was a lawyer with a good track record in lawsuits held in the Senate of Alessandria (the equivalent of today's Court of Appeals). He was elected to the Chamber of Deputies in 1848 and in the tumultuous

---

[11] Massimo D'Azeglio, *Lettere inedited al marchese Emanuele*, Turin 1883.
[12] Francesco Cacciabue, Bartolo Gariglio, Gustavo Mola di Nomaglio, Roberto Sandri Giachino, Sandro Gastaldi, *Studi su Urbano Rattazzi, la sua famiglia, il suo paese*, Masio 2008.

governmental changes of that time he was named Minister of Agriculture and later of Education. In December, in Gioberti's cabinet, he was appointed to the Ministry of Justice and under Prime Minister Chiodo, to the Minstry of Internal Affairs. He best represented the government at the time of the defeat in the Battle of Novara. He was seated on the Left but his leadership was a reassuring one. It was different from the stern style of Lorenzo Valerio, who was sanguine and impulsive: he always appeared to be angry and bent on destroying the world. Rattazzi defined himself and his men (Carlo Cadorna, Domenico Buffa, Giuseppe Cornero, and Giovanni Lanza) as the "third party."[13] Even the moderates found themselves divided into three parts: on the extreme right sat Solaro della Margherita, then came Balbo who was the head of twenty-five deputies who opposed the laws proposed by Siccardi, while Thaon di Revel and his followers expressed their perplexities about issues dealing with free trade.

The opportunity to make a name for themselves presented itself with a law regarding the press. They needed to examine an article that stated that offences made to a foreign head of state could be disputed by a magistrate without passing through the chancellery of the offended country. Napoleon III imposed this article and everyone understood that accepting it meant submission to France. The Left was furious. In Parliament, the deputies Tecchio and Pescatore accused the government of subjugation to foreign power. The *Gazzetta del Popolo* gave voice to the feelings of discontent amongst the journalists. It published an editorial claiming that "Our liberties cast a shadow over Europe." "Today they ask a sacrifice of us. Tomorrow, the will ask for another, and by the same reasoning, you will concede it to them."[14]

Rattazzi knew how to maneuver himself quite well. He announced that he would have voted against the bill but he declared himself open to future collaboration. "If the government," he chose his words carefully, "instead of proposing projects that change

[13] Cesare Perocco, *Vita di Urbano Rattazzi*, Naples 1867.
[14] In *La Gazzetta del Popolo*, February 11, 1852.

our fundamental laws, would try to preserve them and leave them intact then we would all be in agreement and offer our support." Cavour supported him. He contemporaneously defended freedom of the press and the law that placed a limit on its freedom and added that "the Minister should have expected to lose the weak support that it had been receiving for some time from the honorable Menabrea and his political supporters." Prime Minister D'Azeglio, who was absent at the time, knew that a plot to overturn the government was underway as soon as he read it in the newspapers.

They went behind the backs of those voters who voted Cavour to side with D'Azeglio and those that had chosen Rattazzi to assail him; they teamed up and declared an "alliance." It seemed (and still seems) that this was an ingenious political strategy and a betrayal of the will of the people.

Cavour proposed Rattazzi for the position of vice Premier over Mameli, who had been the choice of the conservatives. A few months later, after he had substituted Pinelli who had died, he was elected Prime Minister and won over Boncompagni, who was supported by D'Azeglio, and Tecchio who, in turn, was supported by the radical left.

This crisis was becoming unbearable. Massimo D'Azeglio resigned but was assigned the task of forming a new government that he presented without including Cavour and Farini. The majority was too fragile. This government hardly possessed the power it required to survive and it could not even survive with mouth-to-mouth resuscitation.

The era of Cavour began and he maintained his position as Prime Minister for a long period of time (as compared to his predecessors) but with an extraordinary amount of movement of ministers that came and went from his cabinet.

History narrates that Count Camillo was the one who "wove" the fabric of our country and this is sufficient to ensure his place in the pantheon of the Fathers of Our Country. Nevertheless, the conditions of Piedmont, while the politicians worried about expanding its institutions to the rest of Italy, began to worsen.

At the beginning of each Parliamentary year, the press issued a report detailing the year's legislative activity. Each year these reports were no big affair.

It became necessary to re-evaluate the justice system. Francesco Ferrara noted that the other states could not accept the moral supremacy of Piedmont while its penal code remained more punitive and less refined than theirs. In Tuscany and in the Two Sicilies, the penal code was considerably more modern. Cavour himself was forced to admit that some of the prisons in Piedmont were in a deplorable state. Lord Vernon visited the Sardinian prisons and offered extremely negative comments, though not quite as negative as those of Gladstone who claimed that the Bourbon prisons were the "negation of God." The mortality rate in the prisons of Alessandria was extremely high and a simple prison sentence amounted to a death sentence. In Genoa, the inmates could not even stand because the ceilings were too low.

Angelo Brofferio, while comparing the executions in 1853 in Napoleon III's France with those of Cavour's enlightened Piedmont, verified that the numbers were 45 to 28. "However, the population of France is eight times that of Piedmont and when the proportions are calculated, it is as though in the Kingdom of Sardinia the executions were 224. From 1851 to 1855, there were 113 executions: the mortality rates have increased enormously."[15]

We were in dire need of structural reforms that were not even being taken into consideration.

---

[15] Massimo Viglione, *op. cit.*

CHAPTER 11

The "Boiled Potato" General, the "Black Eunuch," and the "Half-Madman"

In November of 1857, the general elections were held. Cavour's liberals should have been able to win by a landslide, but the candidates were so certain of their success that they underestimated their duties, wasted votes, and wound up receiving blows from all sides. Solara della Margherita and the clericalists established an organized electoral system and were careful to present only one candidate for each electoral college. One bishop presented himself at the polling station with a procession of two hundred clergy members. Solaro was elected in the first round of voting in four polling stations and he won in the second round in three other polling stations.

Cavour won the majority by a very narrow margin and he was the only member of the government to conquer his seat in the first round of voting. La Marmora was defeated by a landslide. Lanza and Rattazzi had to fight to get past the tie-breaker round. Cavour admitted that had this occurred in another, more stable, moment he would have been forced to resign.[1]

Instead, when the Chamber convened, one deputy out of four found the validity of his election questioned. The reasoning waffled from being sound to frivolous. Several months were required to ascertain the validity of the questioned elections. This was just the time that Cavour needed to govern without Parliament's control and to help some undecided member of the Chamber choose a position.

---

[1] Denis Mack Smith, *Cavour, il grande tessitore dell'unità d'Italia*, cit.

The most delicate matter concerned the clergy. By law, they could not be elected but, up until that time, that law had been interpreted in the sense that non-resident clergy members could participate to elections and therefore could have access to the Parliament. When the elections of 1857 saw 9 clergymen elected to the Chamber of Deputies, this law was reinterpreted in a stricter sense. This was a blatant retroactive manipulation of a law, speaking of laws created explicitly for or against specific persons.

With another entirely arbitrary speech, he decided to annul any election in which a clergy member had exercised "moral pressure" and "illegitimate use of spiritual means." One could not prevent a priest from voting but if he used his authority to influence his parishioners then he had an unfair advantage. Of course such a manipulation of conscience was impossible to prove and, in any case, if one admits the possibility that the Church had attempted to convince its followers to vote in a certain manner, it was really only an attempt to even the score, given the moral pressure exercised by the ministers towards their employees, who were threatened with the prospect of losing their jobs if they did not support the suggested candidate.

Which of the two influences was more serious? Which one was more efficient in ensuring that the "proper" name was dropped into the ballot box?

There was nothing to be done: "spiritual pressure" was forbidden and that 10% of elected deputies found themselves with no seat.[2] The conservatives protested: behavior of this type generally did not take the Statute and the constitution seriously. Everyone fell silent.

In that tumultuous period, Rattazzi lost his seat as well. A journalist spit in his face,[3] under the arcade of *Via Po*. A scandal surfaced according to which Rattazzi, during the elections, supported neither the independent liberal candidate (Boggio) nor the ministerial candidate (Count Castellamonte). Instead, he had sup-

---

[2] *Ibidem.*
[3] Adriano Viarengo, op.cit.

ported the clericalist Giuseppe Ponzetti. As an avid proponent of the law on the convents, this was entirely incomprehensible. Cavour, who had utilized his support on numerous occasions, did not defend him. It was Cavour himself who had once said that friendships could not exist in politics. He offered Rattanzi no recognition and no solidarity: he fired him instantly and obliged him to abandon the ministry.

Rattazzi wished to diffuse the information that he had voluntarily left his position but it became common knowledge that he was asked to leave. The "alliance" dissolved and its components went their own separate ways.

After the armistice of Villafranca, Cavour was the one who submitted his resignation. La Marmora took his place and dragged Rattazzi back into the government as Minister of Internal Affairs. This was short lived. Victor Emanuel II was happy to not find himself constantly bickering with Cavour, who always expected to be right. The weak government that Cavour had built allowed him to be meddlesome and cause mischief. Foreigners described him as "a schoolboy on vacation" who was facing a freedom with which he was no longer familiar.

This did not last very long. The king was obliged to return to Cavour and beg him to once again take control of the cabinet. His detractors, who had been monitoring the exchanges between the ambassadors and the envoys residing in Turin, sustained that Britain's solicitations should not be considered irrelevant.[4] Italy had just been born and was still small although it was already a country that possessed a monarchy with limited powers.

Seventy-six days passed and a new crisis emerged. Cavour died on June 6, 1861 when he was almost 51 years old.

Some historians have ventured to prove that Cavour was poisoned[5] by order of Napoleon III. It is, however, more likely that God and a fever due to malaria were the ultimate causes of his

---

[4] Denis Mack Smith, *Cavour, il grande tessitore dell'unità d'Italia*, cit.
[5] Giuseppe Buffa, *Cavour avvelenato su mandato di Napoleone III? Codici da Sezzadio, documenti e testimonianze*, Cornate d'Adda 2007.

demise. Certainly, the circumstances surrounding his illness remain cloudy.[6]

In the political sphere there were many contrasting opinions. Some believed that the death of a statesman of that caliber was the greatest injury the country could have faced in that moment[7]. His political intuitions would have been enormously useful in the coming months and his death had left Italy amidst a sea of troubles. Others were less inclined to praise him. They considered his death to be "fortuitous"[8] for his image because he did not live long enough to witness the disasters that were to come and, most of all, could not be considered responsible for them.

The Capuchin monk Giacomo da Poirino disobeyed the Pope, who had called for the political acts against the Church to be repealed, when he performed the last rites on Cavour. He was put on trial for his actions.[9]

Turin, instead, was in mourning. They were under the impression that by losing the man that had guided them in those years, they would have lost their prestigious role and the opportunities that that barrel-shaped man who loved sauces so much had procured for them.

Everyone had the impression that the uncertain future would be riddled with tribulations.

Who would they nominate to take his place?

Bettino Ricasoli seemed to be the most ideal candidate for his reputation earned during his term in the government of Tuscany. His most powerful weapon was his arrogance. They called him the "Black Eunuch"[10] because he was tall and thin and always wore a tight-fighting coat with tails that made him look even thinner.

This choice revealed itself to be a disappointment. His mistakes cost him to lose the government's support along with his arro-

---

[6] Vittorio Turletti, *Il conte Camillo Benso di Cavour*, Turin 1910.
[7] Rosario Romeo, *Cavour e il suo tempo*, Bari 1977.
[8] Annabella Cabiati, *op. cit.*
[9] Lorenzo Greco, *Il confessore di Cavour*, San Cesario di Lecce 2010.
[10] Alesssandro Orlandini, *Il fantasma di Bettino. Genesi di uno spettro: la leggenda del barone Bettino Ricasoli*, Milan 1988.

gance, which caused him to look down upon all of the other ministers. In this manner his scant knowledge of politics and the mediocrity of his attempts in politics could not justify his errors. He refused to listen to his collaborators and he became annoyed when they attempted to explain matters with which he already should have had some familiarity. He would then proceed to make spur of the moment decisions, which resulted in a great deal of troubles that other people were forced to remedy.

His nomination was vigorously supported by Marco Minghetti who was repaid, so to speak, with the role of Minister of Internal Affairs. This Tuscan-Emilian alliance lasted only for a short time. After ninety days, Minghetti resigned and proceeded to distance himself from a cabinet whose views he no longer shared.[11]

Ricasoli was unable to continue alone and wound up becoming a flash-in-the-pan in the political arena. He was called to head the government on June 12, 1862 and was forced to resign on February 28, 1862 without even calling for the Parliament's majority support.

Urbano Rattanzi took his place. He was chosen thanks to a serious of ambiguous ties he shared with the Savoy monarchy. When he was Minister of Internal Affairs, he managed to cover up a sex scandal that had involved the king. Then Rattazzi had married Maria Letizia Bonaparte Wyse, the cousin of Napoleon III and lover of Victor Emanuel II.[12]

This "family" investiture resulted in a very weak government.

In this extremely delicate moment, when the South was revolting, the King and his Prime Minister believed that they could apply force on international diplomacy by repeating what had been done to the Kingdom of Two Sicilies on Rome.

If Cavour had been able to charm the European diplomats and managed to deny to one party what they had promised to the other, why not try once again?

---

[11] Roberto Martucci, *op. cit.*
[12] *Ibidem.*

Garibaldi arrived in Palermo and began recruiting volunteers. He instigated towns full of people and attended banquets. People arrived from all over Italy with rusty rifles, but what did it matter? They did not have decent rifles in Calatafimi or Volturno. It seemed as though they were rehearsing a script that they had already performed and experimented with ministers who officially denied what they clandestinely encouraged.

But this time Napoleon III did not allow them to pass to easily. He ordered reinforcements to the French troops in Rome and on the borders of the Vatican State. He warned that a war was brewing with the newly formed Italian state.

What could be done? The government, in a state of panic, was forced to disavow Garibaldi, this time officially and unofficially. It declared a state of siege and called for the dissolution of the volunteer troops. Anyone who disobeyed would be arrested without questioning.[13]

On the Aspromonte, they were singing: "Garibaldi was wounded! He was wounded in the leg! Garibaldi is the commander! Garibaldi is the commander of his troops!"

Victor Emanuel II, out of his own initiative, through the offices of the ambassador Terenzio Mamiani, had launched his own destabilization attempt in Greece, to ensure his own son the throne. The French and English opposition grounded the attempt.

Rattazzi resigned on December 1, 1862. He left his post after a terrible fight with the king, which Giacomo Durando witnessed. It seems that they each accused each other of possessing too adventurous a spirit. They were both right.

Sir James Lacaita commented to Lord Gladstone: "His cabinet will be remembered for its absolute lack of respect for any constitutional and moral principle. From the beginning to the end, it was nothing more than a procession of corruption and intrigue without precedent in the Parliamentary history of Piedmont."[14]

---

[13] Stefano Jacini, *Il tramonto del potere temporale*, Bari 1931.
[14] Charles Lacaita, *Un italo-inglese: sir James Lacaita senator del Regno d'Italia*, Manduria 1983.

May the next candidate step forward! Luigi Carlo Farini was instated on December 8, 1862 and was already seriously ill. His youth, passed as a *Carbonaro*, was constantly faced with maintaining secrecy and he lived in the fear of betrayal. This lifestyle had taken a serious toll on his health.[15] He suffered from severe psychological problems that seriously compromised his reasoning. In other words, he was already half-mad.

"He used to stare out at nothing," stated Gaspare Finali, "with his eyes wide open, and he never spoke."[16] This was the ideal situation for the King who wanted to rule without having to deal with any obstacles. The Ministry of Foreign Affairs was offered to the unknown senator Giuseppe Pisolini and the Internal Affairs Ministry went to a Tuscan businessman of questionable dealings, Ubaldino Peruzzi. Minghetti returned to the government as Minister of Finance.

Victor Emanuel, this time, thought of the Veneto region. The plan that he had devised could be assigned to Istvan Stefano Turr, a Hungarian exile who had also been one of the *Mille* soldiers and who had then married the sister of Rattazzi's wife. She was also part of the king's entourage of lovers. With his origins and knowledge, he would have had to incite the provinces along the Danube to bring Austria to a crisis and force it to weaken its Western borders and thereby allowing Italy to make its move. On the verge of an international crisis, an incident occurred that resolved the matter. Farini went completely insane and took a letter opener to the King's throat ordering him to declare war on Russia. It was pointless to insist otherwise. The Prime Minister needed to be hospitalized and quickly. He had survived three months. They sent him to a mental institution in Piedmont, Novalesa, where he remained for a few years without recognizing anyone and without being recognized. Only Lodovico Frapolli, a grandmaster Mason,

---

[15] Franco Della Peruta, "I democratici italiani, i democratici tedeschi e l'unità d'Italia," in *Annali dell'Istituto GG Feltrinelli*, 1960.
[16] Gaspare Finali, *Memorie*, Faenza, 1955.

remembered him and published a moving memoir in his memory in 1894.[17]

On March 22, 1862, Marco Minghetti presented his new government. He was the protagonist of two important laws: the proclamation of a state of siege, and the subsequent ratification of the famous "Pica Law" and the "September Agreement," under which the French agreed to leave Rome with the agreement that Italy would move its capital from Turin to Rome and therefore putting an end to any further annexations of the Church's territories.

Turin found itself demoted to a mere capital of a province, as had previously happened to Milan, Parma, Florence and Naples. There were numerous protests. A great error was made in assigning the maintenance of public order to Morozzo della Rocca, who was the chamberlain of the king. His ineptitude went hand in hand with his reputation as an incompetent bungler. What ensued was a massacre:[18] fifty-one dead and one hundred wounded. The soldiers were all new recruits and therefore had no experience and the *carabinieri* were cadets who also had little experience.

Who began firing first? A shot rang out and the armed forces, whose nerves were frayed, began firing at eye-level. A group of citizens that was in the town square protesting (peacefully) were caught in the cross-fire and even the soldiers and *carabineri* wound up shooting each other. Seeing their neighbors injured only served to increase fear and anger. The armed forces no longer listened to orders and allowed themselves to only follow their instincts which, in moments where it would be absolutely necessary to remain calm, were absolutely wrong.

Victor Emanuel had already earned the nickname of "Bomb King." Minghetti learned that he had resigned upon reading the "*Gazzetta Ufficiale*" but he accepted the exoneration gracefully on September 28, 1864.

---

[17] Lodovico Frapolli, *Quadri storici degli ultii anni dettati dall'auture di "una voce,"* Turin 1894.
[18] Domenico Quirico, *Generali. Controstoria dei vertici militari che fecero e disfecero l'Italia*, Milan 2006.

136

These are episodes in history, which one would rather forget, and yet they did happen. Just like when Victor Emanuel II abandoned Turin, literally escaping like a thief, and reaching Florence before his court after the officials of the city council (rightfully) refused to attend the royal reception that had been organized.

The sixth Prime Minister in four years was Alfonso Ferrero La Marmora who, up until that time, passed his time between the Savoy court and the military barracks.

He was part of that military world that belonged to those more interested in financial gains rather than those who implemented strategies. The Savoy army was a closed environment that was founded upon rigid doctrines and hierarchies. It had a very rich past but a very poor future. The dialect of Turin was a tie that automatically defined a person and distinguished them. They presented themselves as a race of warriors on horseback. They tried to pass themselves off as the Prussians of Europe without allowing themselves to be intimidated by decorations, adjectives, and exclamation marks. If one consulted the annals of the region, one would discover that their most recent days of glory dated back to that "iron-headed" Emanuel Filbert who had sought his glory under the Emperor.

The other Savoys were known more for their ability to manage to free themselves from difficult situations rather than for military valor. They were also known for betraying their neighbors, France and Spain. In the middle of a battle, they were apt to change sides, even when their miserably scant troops could have been decisive.

The Savoy dynasty always seemed to have a spare general when it came to resolving tricky situations. Victor Emanuel III always relied on the infamous Badoglio. Victor Emanuel II kept La Marmora on hand. In 1849, when he had been freshly made king after the abdication of Charles Albert, he found that he had to deal with a revolt in Genoa. The people there had proposed to absurdly continue the war. In the region of Liguria, a general was sent that proceeded to place cannons in the hills and bombarded the city for two days. His exploit would be equaled only by Fiorenzo Bava Beccaris who surrounded the piazzas in Milan, where some workers had united to beg for food and jobs, and proceeded to open fire and kill everyone. Each of these valorous men received the highest honor from the Savoy family for their heroic actions: the *Annunziata* collar. In Turin, two streets are named after them and they are rather close to the center of the city. It would be difficult to petition to change those street names now that the Left, like some monarchists were more realist than the king himself, has become more in favor of the *Risorgimento* than those who were avid supporters of the moment.

What else could have been expected from the officials of that time?

For those of a higher rank, the most complex military training sessions were held in Venaria, at the *Moro* restaurant where Lucia served all of her dishes with a smile.

Those of a lower rank had to manage with the more modest commodities available at the *Cavallo Bianco*, which offered less complex dishes but at a better price.

What was their most famous dish? Boiled potatoes.[19] It was necessary to stab a slice with one's knife with one's left hand. The first one to let the sliced potato slide was forced to pay the bill.

With such hypocritical leaders, the State could not help but project an image of extreme fragility. It always appeared to be on the brink of implosion due to the insurrections in the South and of its blatant administrative ineptitude.

The foreign envoys were never certain whom to talk to in order to receive reliable information.

The patriots did not have words to comment that horrendous disaster.... "Poor Italy...!"

---

[19] *Ibidem.*

CHAPTER 12

The Church under Attack and the Extremists of the Risorgimento

The first thing that the Italian-Piedmontese did upon entering Rome was to call a locksmith to force the locks of the *Quirinale* Palace. The palace had been the residence of the pope who, upon retiring to the Vatican, closed the enormous doors of the palace and took the keys with him. It was necessary to saw off the chains to free the enormous doors.[1]

The second decision was to authorize the construction of two Protestant churches in Rome. This was equivalent to building a mosque in front of St. Peter's or building a Christian cathedral in front of the Mohammed's black rock in Arabia.

What could justify this haste?

How many Protestants were present in Pius IX's Rome?

What was the need to establish a location and meet the demands of an autonomous cult's religious needs?

Perhaps some historians exaggerate when they say that within the *Risorgimento* was a plot against the Church that included the participation of the Evangelicals, English, and the Masons, together to take away the Pope's power.[2] They not only wanted to intervene upon the Pope's temporal power, which effectively was not worth much but through its privation, the spiritual prestige it exerted on millions of loyal followers.

It is probably the heatedness of a debate that would prompt some to interpret certain episodes of the Italian independence movement as an attempt to establish an "anti-Catholic dictatorship."[3]

---

[1] Antonio Di Ierro, *L'ultimo giorno di papa re: 20 Settembre 1870, la breccia di porta Pia*, Milan 2007.
[2] Angela Pelllicciari, *Risorgimento da riscrivere: liberali e massoni contro la Chiesa*, cit.
[3] Antonio Socci, *La dittatura anticattolica. Il caso don Bosco e l'altrqa faccia del Risorgiento*, Milan 2004.

But in that period the Church was subjected to Nero-style persecutions and was indicated as a potential obstacle to the Unification of Italy that needed to be destroyed. In reality, the Church was not contrary to the unification of the country. In the beginning, it was actually favorable but as the movement developed, it began to distance itself due to the methods that were being implemented and the results that it obtained. These were in obvious contradiction to what had been proposed in the beginning of the movement.

Anticlericalism had some particularly grotesque aspects. Giuseppe Garibaldi believed the Pope to be a cubic meter worth of compost and the patriotic meetings he held were an opportunity to hurl a series of insults towards the Catholic hierarchy. A group of hotheads wanted to take advantage of the funeral of Pope Pius IX to attack the followers and to toss the casket into the Tiber River. The bookstores were filled with books that had a cardinal willing to commit a series of vile deeds including, of course, raping the most beautiful girls, making them pregnant and then ignoring the children who were born. It was all folklore.

Cavour's project was far more subtle. He proposed to build an institution where "a free Church could exist in a free State." This declaration appears acceptable at first and even captivating. In actuality, the program hid a clever ruse.

The words that Cavour pronounced allowed the listener to believe that he intended to create harmony between two institutions and allow them to establish a dialogue amongst equals. Instead, what Cavour truly wanted to do was to establish a hegemony in which one of the institutions remained in subordination to the other.

Each "thinker" brought his own small rock to build the wall of anticlericalism.

Bernardo Spaventa, for example, was an exile from the South who lived in Turin.[4] He had far too much anger in his body and

---

[4] Bernardo Spaventa *La libertà d'insegnamento. Una polemica di settant'anni fa* (edited by Giovanni Gentile), Florence 1920.

he stated: "We want freedom of education." It would be difficult to maintain the contrary … from liberals….

"But," he added, "we believe that in order for this to take place, two conditions must be met. The State can choose to recognize this, according to its judgment, or not and evaluate the consequences. A State like Piedmont cannot allow itself the luxury of being fundamentally free until society is not as ideologically homogenous as the State."

Pasquale Mancini was more honest: "Scholastic pluralism is a right but in Italy we oppose this because if we were to apply this notion, it would mean consigning the scholastic system to the Catholics."

The Church could not obtain the recognition of that autonomy that the State claimed only for itself.

The State established its own freedom and placed limitations on the freedom of others: too much for one and little (next to nothing) for the other. The State's power was growing quickly and soon it included all aspects of public and social life. The Church began to see its power relegated to smaller and smaller corners until it ultimately found itself in a very marginal position.

In the summer of 1854, Urbano Rattazzi, who in that period was the Minster of Grace and Justice, ordered the requisition of several monasteries with the pretext that they were needed to quarantine those with cholera. The buildings were cleared much like a house by robbers. Vittorio della Torre protested: "The Minister of Justice wrote three letters to the superiors of the convents ordering them to abandon their homes on a given day by a certain hour otherwise they would be expelled by the public enforcement. There is only one other country where something similar might occur: Turkey. The Sultan's letters and those of the vizier can act as laws. However, the Turkish government is not a constitutional government."[5]

---

[5] Angela Pellicciari, *L'altro Risorgimento, una Guerra di religion dimenticata*, op. cit.

Certainly the operation that confiscated even more of the Church's property was more open-minded.

Cavour was an avid supporter of the right of free association and of the sanctity of private property. However, since the matter pertained to the Church's property, he had no problem departing from his convictions. With a bizarre arrogance, Count Camillo Benso maintained that many convents had made poor use of the legacies that they were to administer. He believed that the meditative orders were "radically useless" and that the mendicant orders gave a bad example to the rest of society because they assumed the roles of beggars. He believed that both represented a serious "obstacle for social progress."

The most valid argument that the government could offer was also its weakest. Each year the government paid the curia a tax of 928,412 lira, which for the crumbling city of Turin was an important sum of money. They preferred to save this money. The Bishop of Casale Monferrato, Luigi Nazario of Calabiana, who was a liberal and a friend of the King, proposed to resolve this problem at its root. The tax could very easily be canceled and the curia could collect that money in another manner. Cavour became furious and declared that it was necessary to "minimize the chances that a dirty plot could ruin the entire country."[6]

The Augustinians disappeared (they wore socks but no shoes) along with the Carthusians, the Benedictines from Cassino, the Cistercians, Olivetans, Oblates of Santa Maria, the Passionists, the Dominicans, Mercedarians, the Children of Mary, fathers of the Oratory, Filippines, Clarisses, Carmelites, Tertiaries, Franciscans, and the Baptistines.

They had already kicked the Jesuits out previously.

They suppressed 334 monasteries and convents and expelled 5491 members of the clergy. They intervened in 65 chapters and 1700 "benefits" that struck another 2099 other institutions and 7871 people.

---

[6] Antonio Socci, *op. cit.*

The economic result did not justify a revolution of that caliber. The State believed that it could raise five million, but it only received three. The majority of the benefits went to those who speculated upon those properties and purchased them at one fifth of their true value.

Was the bishop expected to stay silent throughout all of this? Luigi Fransoni prepared a memorandum for all of the clergy with a series of instructions on how to behave, but before he had a chance to send it out, the police broke into the typographer's studio and broke all of the printing presses.

A throng of young men attacked the Palace of the Curia shouting "Death to Fransoni!!"and "Be gone, pontifical legate!!" Rocks were thrown at the windows and the doors were kicked in. The Salesian historian Giovanni Battista Lomoyne narrates: "A throng of young immigrant patriots that were solicited by the government and paid and instigated by agitators ran throughout the city streets, cursing at the clergy and singing: "Long live Siccardi!"

The Church had become a target for any ill-intentioned person. The right to abuse the Church appeared implicit.

In 1857, "in less than twenty days, seven Churches were devastated in the most sacrilegious of ways: their tabernacles were violently broken." The Bishop of Ivrea, Luigi Moreno, was obliged to make amends. He turned to the priests and ordered them to no longer leave gold and silver objects upon their tabernacles. Furthermore, to avoid that these objects wind up in the hands of thieves, he ordered "the sale of all of the sacred vessels." Minister Rattazzi , nonetheless, found something to complain about: he had stripped the Church of all that was possible but he was still unhappy because he believed that those sales "impoverished the communities followers."[7]

Perhaps D'Azeglio was right when he stated that it was sufficient to attack a priest to deserve a knight's cross.

---

[7] Angela Pellicciari, *L'altro Risorgimento, una Guerra di religione dimenticata*, op. cit.

Don Giacomo Margotti, belligerent founder of the newspaper *L'Armonia* attempted to tally all of the abuse that the Church and its clergy were subjected to. "The archbishop of Pisa has been arrested and taken to Turin where he has been a prisoner for over a month. The Bishop of Faenza, being ill, is under house arrest. The Vicar of Bologna, Monsignor Ratta, has been condemned to three years in jail and fined two thousand lira. To this day, he is still a prisoner. Out of twenty-eight clergy members in the parish of Piacenza, twenty-one have been exiled without a trial or a conviction. The Bishop of Parma was forced to flee from his diocese and his coat of arms was burned in the town square. Cardinal Baluffi, the Bishop of Imola, was tossed into prison."

The justifications for such intense actions were scarce.

"In Chiavari," continued Margotti, "a parish priest was imprisoned for having commented on a memorandum issued by his bishop while he was on the pulpit. The Bishop of Carpi was also imprisoned along with six other parish priests from his diocese. The Minister of Education closed the seminary in Piacenza. A memorandum was issued against many priests and teachers from Piedmont who did not celebrate freedom by singing the *Te Deum*. For the same reason, six teachers who were priests in the Faenza area and several professors from Bologna and Parma were targeted as well." Things were even worse for a Sardinian parish priest named Glielarga who, on the day that the Statute was issued, considered a national holiday, chose to sound the death knells.

"The Camillian Fathers of Ferrara were accused, imprisoned, and declared innocent but nevertheless, exiled to Tuscany. The Sisters of the Sacred Heart were forced to abandon first Milan and then Parma. On the May 25th, two Jesuit priests from Turin were searched and imprisoned along with two Jesuit priests from Genoa. In Mondovì, Father Manera, a professor emeritus in the college, was relieved of his position when he refused to sing. Always on the 25th, a priest in Casalmaggiore was arrested along with one in Modena and another in Ravenna. The priest from Ravenna was the parish priest of the church of Saint Simon and Judah. On May 27th, in Forlì, the Dominican friar Reginaldo Barbiani was arrested.

An attempt was made to arrest the extremely zealous parish priest from Casalpusterlengo, but the local farmers intervened and the police were forced to let him go free. On May 28th, the rectors Bibola and Posara were incarcerated. The parish priest of Cunardo, a Capuchin monk from Genoa, and a poor friar from Modena are all in prison. I lack the patience, but not the facts, to continue."[8]

In that context, only a small percentage of Catholics accepted the challenge and chose to fight for their faith, in defense of their religion with the means at their disposal. Everyone else, in the attempt to simplify matters, divided themselves into two currents of thought. A large portion of them closed themselves inside their homes, offended by the abuse inflicted upon their religion, but limited themselves to witnessing the events in a personal and, in some cases, private manner. This was entirely useless. The others attempted to take the path of dialog but were careful in offering their personal reasons while making the effort to comprehend the reasons of others. This was damaging.

After one hundred and fifty years, history once again presents us with themes that are similar. The values of Christianity and of Western Civilization are being questioned by the ever-growing presence of immigrants that come from an Islamic world and that profess their faith. What rapport can we hope to have with these new citizens? The key word seems to be "tolerance" and this would all be well if it were not a one-way street, like the freedom that the State possessed as compared to that of the Church during the days of the *Risorgimento*.

Too many people behave as if our "tolerance" should consist of watering down our own principles to the point where we hide them in order to preserve them while "their" tolerance presents itself with the arrogance of those who impose their traditions and customs to transform them into values that are universally accepted.

---

[8] Giacomo Margotti, in *Civiltà Cattolica*, June 30 1860.

In this manner, teachers from the kindergarten level try very hard to celebrate Christmas without Baby Jesus because they fear, who knows why, that a small child born in a stable and laid to rest in hay could somehow offend the susceptibility of those who do not believe in the mystery of the Nativity. In compensation, no one must touch Ramadan because it is sacred and therefore must be respected, and one must almost participate in it.

The proximity of different traditions could allow for enrichment (even at a cultural level) with the condition that they consider each other on the same level and with the attitude of establishing a dialog. If Italy must concede the license to build mosques, then there should be a license issued to build Catholic Churches in the Arab world as well. Instead, there is no reciprocity and therefore there is no equal level, which would be an indispensable condition to establish a constructive and proper rapport. The Catholics that live in countries that are primarily Islamic are forced to live in hiding, in catacombs, like during the times of the Roman persecution. For some time now, it appears that their situation has even worsened.

Obviously it would be superficial to make generalizations. Islam is an interesting religion that deserves respect and certainly not all of the loyal Muslims are extremists. A moderate Islam that is open to dialog does exist, but where is it? Who is accepting to co-exist and propose respect, true respect, of each other's culture when they speak? Up until now the only discussions that have emerged are those of angry Imams who consider those who do not think like they do to be "infidels" and who promise fire and brimstone to said "infidels." Can Western Civilization pretend that nothing is happening? How "tolerant" must one be before one is considered stupid and self-injuring?

Are the attacks in Pakistan and Egypt, where Catholics were blown up while they were in their Churches praying to Jesus, sufficient to evoke some concern?

Pope Benedict XVI expressed his solidarity for those Catholics that were massacred for their faith. The Imam of Cairo replied thunderously, "The Pope should not involve himself in matters that concern Egypt!"

The European Parliament diffused an agenda that prudently canceled all Catholic festivities and, you never know, they will calmly lay out an initiative to support freedom of religion.

Too many people, like during the time of the Siccardi Law, protect Islam not because of a positive attitude in their respect, but rather out of prejudice against the Catholic world. It is not a matter of welcoming the followers of Mohammed as much as attacking the Catholic Church.

In this context, it is a waste of effort to be too willing to cooperate because there is no logic in it and it goes beyond common sense. In any country of the world, even the most backward in terms of security, there are laws that regulate immigration. In Italy, we are expected to open our doors and windows to everyone.

The European States are convinced that there need to be some limitations placed on the migratory influx which is quickly becoming unbearable. France was forced to adopt restrictive measures against the nomadic Rom population and in Switzerland,[9] the People's Party proposed a referendum that called for the immediate expulsion of immigrants who have committed crimes.

The Italians are a population of emigrants, it is true. They populated the Americas, from New York to Buenos Aires. They arrived on their tiptoes and they did not raise their voices. They did not ask for anything and occupied their time with their backs bent over their jobs in fields. It is irritating to observe that those who come to your home today do so to claim possession of it and become leaders.

"Zero Tolerance" is a slogan, but its severity is a sign of justice and a guarantee for all good citizens. Even though for some, this expression deserves to be filed under "not politically correct."

---

[9] Livio Caputo, *Referendum "politicamente scorretto."* "La Svizzera vuole cacciare i delinquenti immigrati. Nella Confederazione gli stranieri son oil 22 per cento e commettono il 60 per cento degli omicidi il 57 per cento dei furti. L'UE ha criticato le misure francesi anti-Rom e i respingimenti italiani ma la sicurezza e' un'emergenza ovunque," *Il Giornale*, November 28, 2010.

Oriana Fallaci warned us. Islam does not want to co-exist with Western Civilization: it wants to destroy, colonize, and conquer it. Sometimes even the Catholic Church, often intimidated, confuses solidarity with opportunism and altruism with political choices.

An administrator must be honest but one cannot also ask him to be a saint.

In this vein, it is indispensable to recall an example. On the 11th of November in the fourth century after Christ, Martin, a Roman centurion, found himself on a dirt road on horseback. He stumbled upon a beggar whose teeth chattered from the cold. He had only a few rags of clothing and his shoulders, arms, and legs were uncovered. His skin had already begun to turn purple. Martin felt pity for the beggar and to assist him, he proceeded to cut his own cape in half. He gave the beggar half of his cape.

This episode has entered the annals of Christianity and in the Western calendar because on that day the sun became particularly warm, to the point where it seemed to be summer. Every year, on November 11th, the winter's icy climate, (which is on its way) seems to lessen its grip. A tepid day results in what has become known as "Saint Martin's Summer."

The centurion's gesture was undoubtedly a generous one but certainly careless. In fact, to remedy the situation, the Good Lord was forced to intervene in person with a miracle. Without summer sunshine there most certainly would have been two dead men: the beggar, whose half a cloak would not have been sufficient to cover him and Martin, who with the other half most certainly would not have been able to protect himself either.

Saints rely on miracles. The world of politics that must manage a country has to be careful of the administrative laws it proposes. With respect to immigration, the government must ensure that the statistics are compatible so that hospitality can be assured and that the guarantees it offers the new arrivals are certain. Martin earned Heaven but could certainly not govern even the smallest of communities. Excessive charity can become a boomerang and can transform itself into something dangerous.

ABOUT THE AUTHOR

Journalist and essayist, LORENZO DEL BOCA is the author of numerous books. He worked for many years in Turin where he waspart of the Editorial Committee of *Stampa Sera*. In 1996, he was elected President of the *Federazione Nazionale della Stampa Italiana* (FNSI: *National Federation of the Italian Press*), and in 2001 he was elected President of the Consiglio nazionale dell'Ordine dei giornalisti (*National Board of the Order of Journalists*). His historical writings are dedicated to the Risorgimento period.

He is the author of numerous books translated into several languages. *Maledetti Savoia* (1998); *Il dito dell'anarchico. Storia dell'uomo che sognava di uccidere* Mussolini (2000); *Indietro Savoia! Storia controcorrente del Risorgimento italiano* (2003); *Il Segreto di Camilla* (2005); *Grande guerra, piccoli generali. Una cronaca feroce della prima guerra mondiale* (2007); *L'intermediazione di interessi. Lobbying* (2007; in collaboration with Marcello Menni). *Polentoni* (2011) is his first book translated into English.

In March 2012, he was appointed Register of Sacred Representations of Holy Friday for the town of Romagnano Sesia, in Piedmont.

ABOUT THE TRANSLATOR

ILARIA MARRA ROSIGLIONI is Secretary to the Board of Directors and Special Events Coordinator for ILICA (Italian Language Inter-Cultural Alliance); she currently resides in Rome, Italy. She earned her B.A. in Italian Studies and Art History from Georgetown University. In 2011, Bordighera Press published her English translation of Pino Aprile's *Terroni*.

VIA FOLIOS
A refereed book series dedicated to the culture of Italians and Italian Americans.

Published by Bordighera, Inc., an independently owned not-for-profit scholarly organization that has no legal affiliation with the University of Central Florida and The John D. Calandra Italian American Institute, Queens College/CUNY.

FRED MISURELLA, *Lies to Live by*, Vol. 38, Stories, $15

STEVEN BELLUSCIO, *Constructing a Bibliography*, Vol. 37, Italian Americana, $15

ANTHONY J. TAMBURRI, Ed., *Italian Cultural Studies 2002*, Vol. 36, Essays, $18

BEA TUSIANI, *con amore*, Vol. 35, Memoir, $19

FLAVIA BRIZIO-SKOV, Ed., *Reconstructing Societies in the Aftermath of War*, Vol. 34, History, $30

TAMBURRI, et al., Eds., *Italian Cultural Studies 2001*, Vol. 33, Essays, $18

ELIZABETH G. MESSINA, Ed., *In Our Own Voices*, Vol. 32, Italian American Studies, $25

STANISLAO G. PUGLIESE, *Desperate Inscriptions*, Vol. 31, History, $12

HOSTERT & TAMBURRI, Eds., *Screening Ethnicity*, Vol. 30, Italian American Culture, $25

G. PARATI & B. LAWTON, Eds., *Italian Cultural Studies*, Vol. 29, Essays, $18

HELEN BAROLINI, *More Italian Hours*, Vol. 28, Fiction, $16

FRANCO NASI, Ed., *Intorno alla Via Emilia*, Vol. 27, Culture, $16

ARTHUR L. CLEMENTS, *The Book of Madness & Love*, Vol. 26, Poetry, $10

JOHN CASEY, et al., *Imagining Humanity*, Vol. 25, Interdisciplinary Studies, $18

ROBERT LIMA, *Sardinia/Sardegna*, Vol. 24, Poetry, $10

DANIELA GIOSEFFI, *Going On*, Vol. 23, Poetry, $10

ROSS TALARICO, *The Journey Home*, Vol. 22, Poetry, $12

EMANUEL DI PASQUALE, *The Silver Lake Love Poems*, Vol. 21, Poetry, $7

JOSEPH TUSIANI, *Ethnicity*, Vol. 20, Poetry, $12

JENNIFER LAGIER, *Second Class Citizen*, Vol. 19, Poetry, $8

FELIX STEFANILE, *The Country of Absence*, Vol. 18, Poetry, $9

PHILIP CANNISTRARO, *Blackshirts*, Vol. 17, History, $12

LUIGI RUSTICHELLI, Ed., *Seminario sul racconto*, Vol. 16, Narrative, $10

LEWIS TURCO, *Shaking the Family Tree*, Vol. 15, Memoirs, $9

LUIGI RUSTICHELLI, Ed., *Seminario sulla drammaturgia*, Vol. 14, Theater/Essays, $10

FRED GARDAPHÈ, *Moustache Pete is Dead! Long Live Moustache Pete!*, Vol. 13, Oral Literature, $10

JONE GAILLARD CORSI, *Il libretto d'autore*, 1860–1930, Vol. 12, Criticism, $17

HELEN BAROLINI, *Chiaroscuro: Essays of Identity*, Vol. 11, Essays, $15

PICARAZZI & FEINSTEIN, Eds., *An African Harlequin in Milan*, Vol. 10, Theater/Essays, $15

JOSEPH RICAPITO, *Florentine Streets & Other Poems*, Vol. 9, Poetry, $9

FRED MISURELLA, *Short Time*, Vol. 8, Novella, $7

NED CONDINI, *Quartettsatz*, Vol. 7, Poetry, $7

ANTHONY TAMBURRI, Ed., *Fuori: Essays by Italian/American Lesbians and Gays*, Vol. 6, Essays, $10

ANTONIO GRAMSCI, P. Verdicchio, Trans. & Intro. , *The Southern Question*, Vol. 5, Social Criticism, $5

DANIELA GIOSEFFI, *Word Wounds & Water Flowers*, Vol. 4, Poetry, $8

WILEY FEINSTEIN, *Humility's Deceit: Calvino Reading Ariosto Reading Calvino*, Vol. 3, Criticism, $10

PAOLO A. GIORDANO, Ed., *Joseph Tusiani: Poet, Translator, Humanist*, Vol. 2, Criticism, $25

ROBERT VISCUSI, *Oration Upon the Most Recent Death of Christopher Columbus*, Vol. 1, Poetry, $3